"In a day and age when our so   ry
thought of a personal devil, Mic   at
he is—a liar, deceiver, and accus   so
few give any thought to him today is testimony to his clever and sinister tactics. In *Conquer* we find that he is indeed a 'roaring lion walking about seeking whom he may devour.' But Dr. Youssef reveals that the devil is only able to roar because he has no teeth…the conquering Christ has already defeated him. Devour this book and you will begin to live in the victory that is already yours in Christ."

—**Dr. O.S. Hawkins,** president/CEO, GuideStone Financial Resources

"Dr. Michael Youssef has written an amazing book that helps us to know who our real enemy is. When we are tempted to judge one another or focus on those who have hurt us, Michael shows us not to take things personally from enemies or friends but to know the real culprit—the devil. This book will make you want to pray more, read the Bible more, and know God better. This is Dr. Youssef's best book yet."

—**Dr. R.T. Kendall,** senior minister, Westminster Chapel (1977–2002)

"The war is raging, the enemy is real, but I am grateful that the Bible gives clear truth concerning how we can win the victory. I encourage you to read Michael Youssef's *Conquer* and to understand that we are indeed more than conquerors through Jesus Christ."

—**Dr. Johnny Hunt,** pastor, First Baptist Church, Woodstock, Georgia

MICHAEL YOUSSEF

CONQUER

HARVEST HOUSE PUBLISHERS
EUGENE, OREGON

Cover design by Dual Identity, Inc, Whites Creek, Tennessee

Cover photos © Anne Greenwood, apiguide, aquariagirl1970 / Shutterstock

Published in association with Don Gates of the literary agency, The Gates Group, www.the-gates -group.com

CONQUER
Copyright © 1997, 2015 by Michael Youssef
Published by Harvest House Publishers
Eugene, Oregon 97402
www.harvesthousepublishers.com

Library of Congress Cataloging-in-Publication Data
Youssef, Michael.
[Know your real enemy]
Conquer / Michael Youssef.
pages cm
Previously published: Know your real enemy. Nashville : T. Nelson Publishers, c1997.
ISBN 978-0-7369-5463-1 (pbk.)
ISBN 978-0-7369-5464-8 (eBook)
1. Devil—Christianity. 2. Spiritual warfare. I. Title.
BT982.Y68 2015
235'.4—dc23
2014024349

Printed in the United States of America

15 16 17 18 19 20 21 22 23 / VP-CD / 10 9 8 7 6 5 4 3 2 1

To Phil Cave
whose partnership made it possible for
untold numbers of people around the world
to be set free from Satan's clutches.

Acknowledgments

I am grateful to Don Gates and Lauren Settembrini for using their gifts to help make this book more relevant and practical.

Special thanks to the entire team at Harvest House Publishers—and especially to Bob Hawkins Jr., LaRae Weikert, and Rod Morris, who shared my dream and helped to enlarge the vision of this book.

Finally, thanks to the people of The Church of The Apostles in Atlanta, Georgia, for their constant encouragement and support. They were the first audience for this message, and they helped me to refine the message with their questions and helpful comments.

CONTENTS

PART ONE

KNOW THE ENEMY

CHAPTER 1

WHO IS YOUR REAL ENEMY?

B ob (not his real name) struggled with sexual sin. He had a successful ministry, his wife loved him, and hundreds of others were influenced by his ministry. But he could not resist the lustful glance, could not keep sexual fantasies out of his head.

Carnal desire had gripped him for so long that secretly he had accommodated it. Bob started to pretend it wasn't his fault. He blamed his upbringing. He blamed his psychological makeup. In effect he said, "I don't want to be like this, but what can I do? This is the way I am." Eventually he lost his position after his addiction to pornography was exposed. His ministry was ruined by his failure to overcome sin. He knew it. But he was powerless to stop himself.

At times I am overwhelmed at the number of church people who are addicted to pornography. My friend, Tal Prince, has dedicated his life to helping people who, like himself, were trapped in this modern-day slavery to sin. But that is only one area in which the enemy of our soul has succeeded in invading Christian minds and holding them captive to his powers.

There are other areas of behavior and personality over which some Christians seem to be unable to wrest control back from Satan. As a result, they live second-class lives, dogged by ineffectiveness and guilt. They go around in circles. Typically, they blame their failures on other people or upbringing or circumstances, and they try to fight failure using psychological methods, as though sin could be solved with therapy.

Does it work? Of course not. And for one simple reason. The real *enemy* in sin is not the influence of temperament or other people. The real enemy is the devil.

The same goes for relationships. If you're married, think for a moment about that last tiff you had with your spouse. Probably you felt your partner was in the wrong and felt wounded by your partner's lack of sensitivity and care. At first, arguments like that do little damage because the hurt is more than offset by mutual love and commitment. But it may not stay that way. Have enough arguments and you will find the battle lines being drawn. You begin to anticipate conflict and to see your partner as responsible for your grievances. Sooner or later one of you begins to think, *If only I could get away from this person, my life would be so much better.*

But again, who is the *real* enemy? Whose interests are *really* served when husband and wife start to fight? Not those of the marriage partners, still less those of their children. Only one person wins when marriages break down, and that is the devil. So much hangs on a marriage: the health and security of children, management of the household, effective witnessing, your example to others. All these things Satan can seize and disrupt if he destroys a marriage. That's why marriages are under so much pressure.

> Your soul and your relationships lie at
> the heart of a cosmic conflict. They can
> be won for God or lost to the devil.

Your soul and your relationships lie at the heart of a cosmic conflict. They can be won for God or lost to the devil. So get your priorities straight. Forget your niggling disagreements with the pastor;

forget the way your husband or wife fails to live up to your expectations; forget that other person in the church who constantly gets on your nerves. If you're a Christian, you're fighting the *invisible war*.

THE INVISIBLE WAR

Like all wars, the invisible war has its battlefields.

I stumbled onto such a battlefield while touring Scotland in the early nineties. It was a church in the center of a famous old university town just north of Edinburgh. Like many ancient churches in Scotland, this was an architectural masterpiece and steeped in history. The great Reformer John Knox had once graced its pulpit. Crosses on the street outside marked the sites where Christian believers had been burned at the stake for their faith. Glorious victories had been won here for the gospel. As I stepped inside, I saw a candle burning on the altar and a sparrow flitting about in the roof overhead.

"How many people worship here?" I asked my companion, who lived in the town.

He smiled sadly. "Have a guess."

"Five hundred?" I ventured. By Scottish standards the building was large.

"Try again."

"Two hundred?"

He shook his head. "Come here at eleven next Sunday and you'll see six people in the pews."

"Six?"

"Six elderly ladies. Let me tell you the story behind it."

And this is the story he told me. Twenty years ago the minister and the organist had a falling-out. Neither one can remember now what caused their disagreement. But since that time neither one has spoken a single word to the other. On Sunday morning the minister arrives early and places a list of hymns on the organ. The organist plays them, then leaves by a different door. In twenty years nobody new has joined the church, and slowly the existing congregation has died off.

When I heard that story I was powerfully reminded of Paul's parting words to the Ephesians:

> Pay careful attention to yourselves and to all the flock, in which the Holy Spirit has made you overseers, to care for the church of God, which he obtained with his own blood. I know that after my departure fierce wolves will come in among you, not sparing the flock; and from among your own selves will arise men speaking twisted things, to draw away the disciples after them (Acts 20:28-30).

In that Scottish church, two of the most influential believers had become enemies. But of course neither of them was the *real* enemy. They were members of the same army—the army of God—and theirs was a brawl within the platoon. And a very serious one it was. It had cost the church its membership and crippled God's mission to the unsaved. In the invisible war, that church was vital territory lost to Satan.

Never mind the beauty of the architecture. Never mind the candle or the sparrow flitting around the rafters. When I stepped through those doors, I might as well have been in Prague the day after the Soviet tanks rolled in or in Saigon the day after the Vietcong invaded. The sorry tale of broken relationships and unresolved bitterness hid a deeper, spiritual truth: the church was now in Enemy hands.

Satan dresses up his wolves as sheep,
so that experience and discernment
are needed to identify them.

It is not hard to find other examples of churches lost to the devil. Very seldom are they taken by direct attack. Satan is too clever for that; if believers see him coming, he knows he will be repulsed. So he fights an invisible war. He proceeds by stealth. He dresses up his wolves as sheep, so that experience and discernment are needed to identify them.

Rob Bell founded Mars Hill Bible Church in Grandville, Michigan, in 1999. It quickly became one of America's fastest-growing churches, reaching an average weekly attendance of almost ten thousand people by 2005. However, upon the release of his 2011 book, *Love Wins*, it became apparent that this pastor who founded a "Bible church" did not hold to the teachings found in Scripture.

In *Love Wins*, Bell questions the existence of hell and the truth that only believers in Jesus Christ go to heaven. This controversy created quite a stir in the evangelical community, some immediately labeling Bell a heretic, but thousands more coming to his defense and jumping on the bandwagon of a more "tolerant" god who adapts to our culture.

Rob Bell eventually stepped down as pastor of Mars Hill Bible Church, but his following has only continued to grow. He has gone on to openly affirm same-sex marriage, to the delight of many. His latest book, *What We Talk About When We Talk About God*, is filled with even more false teaching, but it was the first recommended title in "Oprah's Super Soulful Book of the Month" club. It appears that the more Bell waters down the gospel of Jesus Christ, the more accepted he becomes by popular culture. Unfortunately, this "more tolerant" and "less judgmental" god that Bell has created is not the God of the Bible, and is powerless to save.

No congregation is safe. Take an active, vibrant church that seeks to win the lost and equip the saints. One or two individuals come into the church and start to introduce new ideas. They say things like, "We need to move in a different direction. We need to do some social service, some counseling." Gently, and with arguments so subtle it's hard to refute them, they move the whole congregation out of the will of God. As a result, the mix of the membership changes. The original detractors gather more detractors around them, and within a short period of time, the church has become both dead and deadly.

This is undercover work. When those wolves come in they look like sheep, they bleat like sheep, and the sheep befriend them. But the wolves are agents of the Enemy. Whether they realize it or not, they are being used to weaken the church's defenses and destroy it.

So how do we begin to win the invisible war, to keep the wolves at bay?

KNOW YOUR ENEMY!

Archie Parrish, an ex-serviceman and friend of many years, taught me a vital lesson. Archie told me of his experiences in the Korean War. "When I got there, they handed me a brochure. Every American soldier received one of these. It was titled *Know Your Enemy.*"

That brochure, he said, contained everything American soldiers needed to know about the North Koreans. What were they like? How did they think? Where did they attack? What was their ultimate goal? Knowing the answers to such questions would decide whether you won or lost. Any soldier doing a tour of duty in Korea would read and reread that brochure until he could repeat it backward. Knowledge gave strategic advantage; ignorance was death.

The Enemy uses even born-again,
Spirit-filled believers as his emissaries
to destroy the work of God.

Tragically, when it comes to the invisible war, Christians are big on ignorance. Probably not one in ten believers would identify Satan as the real Enemy, much less know how to conquer him. The average Christian is oblivious to spiritual conflict. The average Christian does not possess that vital, lifesaving information on how to overcome Satan and his demonic cohorts. Consequently, the Enemy uses even born-again, Spirit-filled believers as his emissaries to destroy the work of God.

Did you catch what I just said?

If not, read it again. *The Enemy uses believers.* That's exactly what has happened to many Christian leaders. It's exactly what happened between the minister and the organist at that old church in Scotland. And it's exactly what is happening in countless Christian marriages and other Christian relationships the length and breadth of the world. Once the devil has a foothold in your life, he will use it. You fight *in* this invisible war, but the war is also fought *in you.*

You say, "How can the Enemy get into a believer and use him to destroy God's work?" Well, the invisible war is much the same as ordinary war. A soldier in the regular army can easily serve his enemy's purposes, through cowardice, ignorance, inattention, or lack of resolve. Think what you like about the rights and wrongs of Vietnam: There is no denying that one of the reasons America lost in Vietnam was the lack of resolve and commitment on the part of the government leadership to fight to win. Half-heartedness is more serious than retreating.

Think about our lack of resolve in Iraq and where this has gotten us now.

In a similar way, surrendering your life to the lordship of Jesus Christ is not the end of the story. It is a decisive step. By acknowledging that there is no way to salvation except through Jesus, you move from darkness into light. You change your destination from hell to heaven. But you are not yet finished with your journey. You are not yet sanctified. You are like a massive corporation in the aftermath of a takeover—under new ownership, with new objectives, but with many of the old management structures still in place. Salvation takes time to soak in.

I want you to imagine it this way: In your spiritual being you are like a house with many doors. Each of those doors opens onto your soul, and each one needs to be bolted securely to prevent illegal entry. And despite the fact that you have surrendered your life to the Lord Jesus Christ, not all of those doors are locked. If Satan comes up and gives the doors a push, sooner or later he will find one that swings open. Now he has a way into your soul. He has found your Achilles' heel.

In the Middle East, where I grew up, professional thieves don't usually break and enter. They don't *break*, that is. They go around the houses and push on the doors to see if anyone has left his door unlocked, and only then do they go in to steal and rob and destroy. Satan is a gentleman thief. He does not break and enter. If he comes into your life, it is because you have invited him, because one or two of those doors are swinging on their hinges.

This is a subject I will return to in more detail. Be aware now, though, of the number of doors you may be leaving unlocked. Anger is a door. If the door of anger is left unbolted, Satan will enter your life and create havoc in your relationships. Bitterness is a door. Hatred is a door. Lying is a door. Rebellion is a door. Envy is a door. Sexual lust is a door. Greed is a door. False guilt is a door. Shame is a door. Attraction to horoscopes and to fortune-telling and to the occult is a door. Are you understanding me? These doors, if they are not checked and bolted every day, will give the Enemy access to your soul.

> The first step to conquering your
> Enemy is *knowing him.*

And there is another door—the door I want to deal with first. That door is *ignorance*. For the first step to conquering your Enemy is *knowing him.* Know your Enemy. Know how to conquer him before he eats you for lunch, because that's what he wants to do. Know his operational procedure. Know what he thinks. Know when he attacks, how he attacks, where he attacks. Give yourself to the task of intelligence gathering. Any army worth its name remains in a constant state of readiness, alert to its enemy's activities. The army that is well informed can never be overwhelmed by a surprise attack.

All this exhortation to readiness may have you worried. Is our Enemy in the invisible war so stealthy and powerful that we are in constant danger of being overrun? The answer, of course, is no. For one thing, we need to take the long view and remember that the outcome of this war is already decided. No matter how many battles the devil may win, in the end he is going to be vanquished. That means we are the only army in history to be guaranteed success before firing a single shot. Our setbacks against the devil may be painful and costly, but they do not determine the final outcome.

Therefore we should take care to build the right attitude. We are on the winning side. Victory is assured. You may be saying, "I am not afraid of the devil." And that's good. But that is not the central issue. Far more important is *whether the devil is afraid of you.* What have you done lately to scare the devil? What victory have you scored to make him run for cover?

When the great evangelist George Whitefield came to New England, a prominent and blue-blooded Bostonian minister confronted him and said, "Mr. Whitefield, I'm very sorry you came to Boston." To which the evangelist replied, "So is the devil, sir, so is the devil." Great crowds flocked to hear Whitefield, and as a result of his preaching, the boundaries of God's kingdom were significantly extended.

The devil fears his final defeat, which is
why he hates to be reminded of it.

The devil fears his final defeat, which is why he hates to be reminded of it. I was told that an eminent preacher once explained why many Christians refuse to believe in the Bible as the authoritative Word of God. He said, "They call Genesis a myth and the Revelation a mystery." In his opinion, no man was clever enough to come up with objections like this—they sprang from the devil himself. "And the reason the devil is so anxious to get rid of Genesis and Revelation," he said, "is that in Genesis his sentence is declared and in Revelation it is executed."

Let me give you some encouragement. Right now—right this very second—you have the devil on the run. How? Simply because you are taking the time and trouble to do what he most hates to see. You are getting to know your Enemy, uncovering his weaknesses, countering his strengths. For that reason, he will do his utmost to prevent you from finishing this book. And when you have finished it, he will do his utmost to make you forget what it said. So why not make the devil really mad? Go get a notepad and pen, and start writing down what the Spirit of God is teaching you.

In the chapters that follow we will look at a number of crucial and difficult areas. We will learn about the devil's command structures and strategies, his preferred methods of attack, and his ultimate destruction. Before that, though, I want to sketch in some of the background and ask what many people consider to be the biggest question of all: Where did the devil come from?

WHERE DID THE DEVIL COME FROM?

Turn with me to two key biblical passages: Ezekiel 28:11-19 and Isaiah 14:12-15—passages in which we find the most definitive biblical teaching on the origin of Satan.

In these passages neither Ezekiel nor Isaiah addressed Satan directly. Instead their taunts were directed against contemporary leaders whose opposition to God made them types of Satan. God instructed Ezekiel: "Son of man, raise a lamentation over the king of Tyre" (Ezekiel 28:12). Similarly, Isaiah was told: "you will take up this taunt against the king of Babylon" (Isaiah 14:4).

All the enemies of God in the Old Testament were types of Satan, including the pharaoh confronted by Moses. And wherever these types are found, we can be sure the Bible is teaching us something important about the devil. Even today any king, any prince, any president, or any ruler who refuses or rejects God, acts in effect as Satan's personal representative. Any government that rejects God becomes the seat of Satan. Why? Because Satan uses people to accomplish his purpose. Satan always employs willing agents to do his evil bidding.

The first clue to Satan's origins is found in Isaiah's use of the name *Lucifer*:

> "How you are fallen from heaven,
> O Lucifer, son of the morning!
> How you are cut down to the ground,
> You who weakened the nations!"
> (Isaiah 14:12 NKJV)

At first this seems paradoxical. The name Lucifer literally means "light-bearer, the brilliant one, the shining one." Ezekiel affirmed this same truth by picturing Satan dressed in a sort of glitter-suit of precious stones. God said of him:

> "You were the signet of perfection,
>   full of wisdom and perfect in beauty.
> You were in Eden, the garden of God;
>   every precious stone was your covering,
> sardius, topaz, and diamond,
>   beryl, onyx, and jasper,
> sapphire, emerald, and carbuncle;
>   and crafted in gold were your settings
>   and your engravings.
> On the day that you were created
>   they were prepared."
> (Ezekiel 28:12-13)

In contrast to Ezekiel, Paul later described the Ephesians' struggle against "the rulers, against the authorities, against the cosmic powers over this present darkness, against the spiritual forces of evil in the heavenly places" (Ephesians 6:12). How can Satan's realm of darkness be presided over by one who was called the bearer of light?

Remember, we are talking about *origins* here. God created Lucifer to be one of his principal servants. Read further in Ezekiel:

> "You were an anointed guardian cherub.
> I placed you; you were on the holy mountain of God;
> in the midst of the stones of fire you walked.
> You were blameless in your ways
> from the day you were created,
> till unrighteousness was found in you."
> (Ezekiel 28:14-15)

According to Ezekiel, Satan was "the signet of perfection, full of wisdom and perfect in beauty." Even so, Lucifer's light was the light of a mirror, not that of a torch. The light never originated within him. Not one of those precious stones described in Ezekiel 28 could shine by itself; put it in a dark room and you wouldn't even see it. Lucifer shone because he *reflected* the beauty and light of God.

Don't forget that Lucifer was one of the most senior angels. He worked at the highest level. Unlike Moses, who had to cover his face in the presence of God, Lucifer was able to look at God's very throne. He was able to voice praise, to voice adoration, to voice worship to God. Such was his privilege and the authority he had from on high.

This is what makes Satan such a cunning and dangerous adversary. He is like a top-ranking defector from the CIA who knows the protocols and the secret codes, who can pick up his old contacts and be absolutely convincing. For this reason Paul wrote to the Corinthians:

> And what I am doing I will continue to do, in order to
> undermine the claim of those who would like to claim
> that in their boasted mission they work on the same

terms as we do. For such men are false apostles, deceitful workmen, disguising themselves as apostles of Christ. And no wonder, for even Satan disguises himself as an angel of light (2 Corinthians 11:12-14).

Satan knows exactly how to look like an angel
of light, because that is what he was.

Satan knows exactly how to look like an angel of light, because that is what he was. That is what God created him to be: Lucifer. Not because he had any beauty of his own, but because he would so magnificently reflect the beauty and glory of his Creator. And don't miss what Paul wrote about those false apostles "disguising themselves as apostles of Christ." The wolves take after their leader; they are masters of disguise. In a later chapter I will return to this problem and show how effectively, even now, Satan's cohorts are being sent to masquerade as true believers.

Pride Came Before the Fall

But let's look at a second clue to Satan's origins. He was created by the one true eternal God, who has no beginning and no end. As a created being Satan was obliged to offer worship, to offer praise, to adore the Creator God. He was perfect in every way. He was the epitome of wisdom. He was the ultimate in beauty. But he was created for a purpose. God delegated to him full executive responsibility for the angelic hosts who serve him throughout the universe.

The Bible does not tell us how many there are in this host. *Zillions*, today's kids would say. But even zillions seems an underestimate. And within this heavenly host, Paul tells us in Ephesians 1:21, there are numerous ranks, classes, and grades ("rule and authority and power and dominion"). Each rank or class or grade has a different responsibility. Each has a different area of ministry. Each has a sphere of work that is different from the others. Read Revelation and you will find that the job of some angels is to stand constantly before the throne of God, saying,

> "Holy, holy, holy, is the Lord God Almighty,
>   who was and is and is to come!"
>   (Revelation 4:8)

The only thing the Bible says of *all* angels—in Hebrews 1:14—is that they are "ministering spirits."

It seems that Lucifer presided over this entire group. He was the executive VP. And this position brought him awesome power. He acted as top intermediary, chief middleman. He gathered worship from every part of creation and brought it into the presence of God. But being a middleman, even chief middleman, isn't easy. It requires supernatural humility and supernatural maturity.

> For Lucifer to entertain the ambition of replacing
> God was not only blasphemous but irrational.

Ask any top executive. Sure, you know how far you have risen and how many people are down there below you. But the closer you get to the top, the more intensely you desire to climb that final rung and become the undisputed head. In corporate life, perhaps, this is not such an unreasonable ambition; the move from executive VP to CEO is not such a large one. But an unbridgeable gulf separates creature from Creator; consequently, for Lucifer to entertain the ambition of replacing God was not only blasphemous but irrational.

Isaiah gives us insight into Lucifer's thought processes at this point:

> "You said in your heart,
>   'I will ascend to heaven;
> above the stars of God
>   I will set my throne on high;

I will sit on the mount of assembly
  in the far reaches of the north;
I will ascend above the heights of the clouds;
  I will make myself like the Most High.'"
                    (Isaiah 14:13-14)

See the verbs by which Lucifer expressed his ambition:

- I will ascend…
- I will set my throne on high…
- I will sit…
- I will ascend above…
- I will make myself like…

Five times in two verses the same words appear: *I will.* God created Lucifer perfect, but he also created him with the capacity to choose—just as he did Adam and Eve. To have the power of choice is to be, in a special way, aware of yourself as the chooser. It opens the possibility of becoming so focused on yourself that you forget how insignificant you really are.

Holding up your hand in front of your face, you believe your hand to be larger than a mountain on the horizon. You begin to equate yourself with God. And from this fatal perceptual error springs all kinds of evil: self-focus, pride, and false ambition.

> Lucifer failed to recognize that everything
> he possessed was a gift from God, and
> that without God he was nothing.

This is what happened to Lucifer. He became proud of his beauty. He became proud of his intellect. He became proud of his capacity. He became proud of his attainment. He failed to recognize that everything he possessed was a gift from God, and that without God he was nothing. He really thought he deserved worship in his own right. Ezekiel put it well when he, speaking on behalf of the Lord, said to Satan,

> "Your heart was proud because of your beauty;
>   you corrupted your wisdom for the sake of your
>   splendor."
>
> (Ezekiel 28:17)

And that is why God fired him and threw him out of heaven. Jesus referred to this event when he said, "I saw Satan fall like lightning from heaven" (Luke 10:18). Here is Ezekiel's version:

> "In the abundance of your trade
>   you were filled with violence in your midst, and
>   you sinned;
> so I cast you as a profane thing from the mountain of God,
>   and I destroyed you, O guardian cherub,
>   from the midst of the stones of fire.
> Your heart was proud because of your beauty;
>   you corrupted your wisdom for the sake of your
>   splendor.
> I cast you to the ground;
>   I exposed you before kings,
>   to feast their eyes on you."
>
> (Ezekiel 28:16-17)

THREE QUESTIONS AND A WARNING

At this point some Christians find fault with God. Didn't God know from the beginning, they ask, that pride would capture the heart of Lucifer? The answer is yes because God is omniscient, and being omniscient means you know everything ahead of time. So, could God not have prevented Satan's fall? Again the answer is yes because God is also omnipotent. He can do anything. And here comes the third question. If God knew Lucifer would rebel, and if God could have prevented it, why didn't he do so?

Well, why didn't he? On the face of it, preventing Satan's rebellion would have saved an awful lot of trouble. There would have been no fall in Eden, no history of human sin, no need for redemption, no destruction of the present order to make way for the new heavens and new earth.

The closest we can get to answering this question is to point to the importance of free will. Without free will, after all, created beings are only machines. Like computers, they do exactly what they are told to do—no more, no less. It could be argued that we are real persons at all only to the extent that we are free—free even to reject God. Here, though, we are moving out of the circle of biblical certainty and into the realm of speculation.

At this point there is a far more pressing issue to consider. If you forget everything else I've said so far, don't forget what I'm going to say now.

Lucifer's sin has been reproduced again and again throughout history. It was reproduced in Adam and Eve when they believed the serpent's lie and wanted to be like God. It was reproduced when the people of Israel arrived in the Promised Land, only to turn their backs on God and worship Baal. It was reproduced again when the proud Pharisees refused to repent and believe in the Lord Jesus Christ, the real light of God, the only anointed Messiah, and the only Savior. It is repeated every single day when an unsaved person refuses to submit to the authority of God's Son. Lucifer's sin is reproduced again and again. For the unsaved do not want to acknowledge that they cannot know God by their own minds, that they cannot reach God by their good works, that they cannot be saved their own way.

But worse than that, Satan's sin is also being reproduced among believers. This is why the apostle Paul warned Timothy not to let an immature Christian assume a position of leadership. This is not reverse ageism. Paul was not talking about chronological maturity but spiritual maturity. How many Christian leaders have we seen in America in the last twenty years who have been disgraced through their immaturity? Such a person, said Paul, should be kept from leadership responsibility "or he may become puffed up with conceit and fall into the condemnation of the devil" (1 Timothy 3:6).

> So be warned, whoever you are, you are
> never closer to Satan, or more clearly under
> his control, than when pride drives you.

So be warned, whoever you are—man or woman, clergy or layperson, old or young—you are never closer to Satan, or more clearly under his control, than when pride drives you. Pride distorts your judgment. It makes you covet things you have no right to. It alienates you from God. No temptation confronts us more persistently or entices us more subtly than the temptation of pride, because through pride Satan reproduces himself. So let no one "think of himself more highly than he ought" (Romans 12:3)—for to do so is to think as the Enemy thinks.

As you learn about the Enemy, examine yourself for traces of pride—pride of knowledge, pride of achievement, pride of position, pride of possession, even pride in your cleverness at thwarting Satan. Whatever form it takes, pride will always bring you to the doors of the recruiting office where the devil turns sheep into wolves.

Don't let it happen to you.

CHAPTER 2

THE ENEMY:
A SEVEN-POINT PROFILE

A man went to his doctor for a thorough physical examination. Afterward he said, "Doctor, give it to me straight. I can take it. Just tell me what's wrong with me."

"Do you really want to know?" the doctor said.

"Oh, yes. Don't dress it up in fancy language. I want the truth in plain English. What's really wrong with me?"

"Well, there is nothing wrong with you except that you're lazy."

The man thought for a minute and said, "Okay, now give me the medical term so I can tell my wife."

In spite of the man's claim to want the truth in plain English, what he really wanted was to deceive his wife into believing he had a medical condition. *Deception* is one of your Enemy's chief weapons. For instance, see how the book of Revelation describes his fall from heaven:

> And the great dragon was thrown down, that ancient serpent, who is called the devil and Satan, the deceiver of the whole world—he was thrown down to the earth, and his angels were thrown down with him (Revelation 12:9).

The devil *deceives the whole world.* Now think about that. It is quite a feat. Not even the most wily politician could manage it. How does the Enemy succeed? One thing we can see immediately is that Satan, like the perfect salesperson, believes wholeheartedly in his own product. We discovered in the last chapter that Satan thinks he *deserves* the worship due to God. In fact, he has fallen for his own PR. Before deceiving anyone else, he has completely deceived himself. He really believes the falsehoods he peddles to others.

This means we should never expect the Enemy to come clean about deception. He is never going to tap you on the shoulder and say, "Now Mr. So-and-so, now Ms. So-and-so, my name is the devil and today I'm going to deceive you." What would be the point? He is too clever for that. Ninety-nine times out of a hundred you will not even know it's the devil who is tempting you, and it will not even occur to you that you're being tempted.

Sadly, experience in leadership does not always make you resistant to deceit. Over the years too many prominent Christians have shown themselves naive or weak in the face of temptation. That, in short, is why so many mainline churches and so many once-godly schools have strayed from the intentions of their founders. Successive leaders have unwittingly listened to the voice of Satan and taken the institutions entrusted to their care straight into a blind alley.

> Leaders are as vulnerable to deception as anyone else. Perceiving the Enemy's assaults, and countering them, takes a special kind of determination.

This should not surprise us. The Enemy targets Christian leaders, and his purposes are often doggedly pursued by ordained ministers, elders of the church, heads of schools, and presidents of colleges. Leaders are as vulnerable to deception as anyone else. Perceiving the Enemy's assaults, and countering them, takes a special kind of determination.

Paul had this gift. Paul wrote of the Enemy, "we are not ignorant of his designs" (2 Corinthians 2:11). The apostle Paul had the same instinctive grasp of Satan's methods as a seasoned detective might have of the criminal mind. He understood Satan's philosophy. He understood his character. He understood his purpose. He understood his method of operation.

So what traits characterize the Enemy? How can we recognize him? We need to know that, for as long as his disguise remains intact, the Enemy will move among us undetected and unchallenged. He will surprise and ambush us, and inch by inch, soul by soul, relationship by relationship, church by church, invade God's territory in the invisible war.

A PROFILE OF THE ENEMY

In this chapter, then, I want to look at seven facts about the devil. Together they give us an essential profile. Armed with this profile we will know whom we're looking for, we will have a description of him, and we will no longer be fighting a phantom. As you study the Enemy and build up his profile, evaluate yourself for signs of the devil's work in your own life. Have you in any way begun to model your lifestyle on the deceptions of the devil instead of the truths of God? Do you imitate the Enemy of God, or do you endeavor to imitate the Savior of your soul? Do you deceive, slander, and malign, or do you encourage, uplift, and uphold? Read carefully, and think hard.

Fact 1: The Enemy Believes in Questioning Authority

Growing up in Egypt I heard many stories about the Battle of El Alamein, fought during the Second World War on Egyptian soil.

In 1942 the Allies found themselves unable to achieve a decisive victory against Rommel in the Egyptian western desert. Rommel had been nicknamed the Desert Fox because he had so often and so effectively outmaneuvered the Allied forces. Finally, fearing Rommel would outwit them, Churchill sent in Field Marshall Bernard Montgomery to take the Allied command.

Montgomery was an autocratic and persistent general. Churchill called him "indomitable in retreat, invincible in advance, insufferable in victory." He was the man who finally outfoxed the Desert Fox and won the Battle of El Alamein. But how did he do it? The answer is surprisingly simple. Montgomery discovered that under the previous leadership almost every order had been questioned by subordinate officers, all the way down to the lowest ranks. In effect, the Allies had been paralyzed by disagreement. Montgomery immediately put a stop to it. Under his leadership orders were not questioned, debated, or discussed—they were simply obeyed. And in that lay the secret of victory.

> The devil questioned the authority of
> God. And now that he has been thrown
> out of heaven, he likes nothing better than
> to see others doing the same thing.

A similar questioning of orders lies at the heart of the devil's fall. He questioned the authority of God. And now that he has been thrown out of heaven, he likes nothing better than to see others doing the same thing. He wants Christians to be paralyzed, just as the Allied forces were in the war with Rommel—by persistently having them turn a *command* into a *debate*.

If you doubt that, go back to the beginning. Leaf through the opening pages of your Bible and see what happened in the first encounter between humankind and the devil. In particular, look at Genesis 3:1-7, the conversation between the serpent and Eve. We often make the mistake of assuming that Adam and Eve were pushovers. It's not true. Adam and Eve lived in closer communion with God than any of us do today. To topple them, Satan would need to use all his craftiness. How did he do it?

Satan, the serpent, did not confront Eve with the straight truth. He did not say, "Eve, if you obey me instead of God, you and all my fallen angels will wind up in the lake of fire, which has been prepared for us." Nor did he accuse God bluntly of lying. Instead, he led with a question:

> Now the serpent was more crafty than any other beast of the field that the LORD God had made.
> He said to the woman, "Did God actually say, 'You shall not eat of any tree in the garden'?" (Genesis 3:1).

Notice that he turned the command into a debate. In effect he said, "Eve, did God really say it that way? Did you hear it right? Did you really understand him correctly?" Without making any false allegations, he made it possible for Eve to debate the truth of God's word. Notice something else too. The English Standard Version describes the serpent as "crafty." In the Hebrew, though, the literal meaning of that word is "prudent." I think this second translation is the better one. It suggests that the serpent was known not for his wiliness (for why, then, should Eve have believed him?) but rather for his caution and reliability. Eve would have placed the same kind of trust in that serpent as you might place in a judge. He had a good reputation around the Garden. He was not known for rashness.

Nor is there any indication that his speaking to Eve caused her surprise. On the contrary, they seem to have been familiar with each other, almost old friends. When Eve listened to the serpent she was ready to hear wise counsel, common sense, reason. Perhaps, then, it was only by using the serpent that Satan could have broken down Eve's defenses. For she certainly knew the command of God. She knew the will of God. She knew the love of God. She knew the fellowship of God. Not without the greatest care and subtlety could

Satan hope to persuade Eve to exchange divine knowledge for natural reasoning, to make her question the divine command.

But he succeeded. And no sooner had he introduced the possibility of debate than he followed up by arguing, ever so gently, the case for the other side: Would Adam and Eve *really* die if they ate the fruit of the tree?

> But the serpent said to the woman, "You will not surely die. For God knows that when you eat of it your eyes will be opened, and you will be like God, knowing good and evil" (Genesis 3:4-5).

Until this point it had never occurred to Eve that there was another way of seeing the issue. Now, though, she was exposed to another interpretation, an interpretation that not only differed from the first, but also (take note of this) appeared to have logic on its side.

Why is this so important? Because in a debate, the most logical argument is the argument that *wins*. By the way, this is the very argument that the so-called homosexual lobby is using in churches. And what, at first sight, could be more logical than the idea that God had a hidden agenda in putting the tree out-of-bounds—that a bite of the fruit, far from inviting damnation, would lead to growth and enlightenment? Eve looked at the tree and saw that it was "good for food, and that it was a delight to the eyes, and that the tree was to be desired to make one wise," so "she took of its fruit and ate" (Genesis 3:6).

If the Enemy can get you to debate any of the issues that are settled in the Word of God, he's two-thirds of the way through.

In truth, though, Eve was finished long before she looked. She was finished the moment she listened to the serpent's question, the moment she agreed to treat God's command as something to haggle over.

The same applies today. If the Enemy can get you to debate any of the issues that are settled in the Word of God, he's two-thirds of the way through. You're a dead duck. If he gets you to debate the rights and wrongs of cheating on your income tax, he's two-thirds of the way there. If he gets you to debate the rights and wrongs of emotional involvement outside your marriage, he's two-thirds of the way there. If he gets you to debate the rights and wrongs of compromising your faithful walk with God, he's two-thirds of the way there. If he gets you to debate even the possibility that marriage can take place between same-sex couples, he is two-thirds of the way there.

These issues have already been settled in the Word of God. There are plenty of things we can debate legitimately, plenty of areas where careful debate is not only allowable but necessary. But on the core issues of doctrine and morality, God has already spoken, and there is no doubt about what he meant.

Let me give you six examples of issues that should be commands but have turned into debates.

1. Abortion

The Enemy says, "Doesn't God really want every baby born into this world to be a wanted baby?" Accept that, and he's two-thirds of the way to making you a murderer. Why? Because *not* being wanted seems such a terrible fate that by comparison abortion looks like an act of mercy.

> Since when was not wanting someone
> an excuse for killing them?

Millions of babies are murdered each year in America because they are "not wanted." But since when was not wanting someone an excuse for killing them? God's command is clear: "You shall not murder."

2. Infidelity

The Enemy says, "Doesn't God want everyone to be happy?" Accept that, and you're two-thirds of the way to getting a divorce. *Happiness* is a magic word in America. Everyone wants to be happy. Everyone feels it's their right. So what happens if you're not happy, if your marriage is making you miserable?

Often the Enemy will put an easy solution in your way. He points to someone and whispers, "That woman over there, that man over there. If you want happiness, break free from your spouse and start again." Now I'm not denying that a marriage can end up in a heartbreaking mess, but if you put happiness before everything else, you will not only persuade yourself into a divorce, you will probably wreck your next relationship too. That's how the Enemy works.

3. The Bible

The Enemy says, "Surely a loving God would prevent suffering." Accept that, and you're two-thirds of the way to undermining the authority of Scripture. The histories contained in the Bible are full of suffering and wars and inhuman cruelty. It is a fact that, in his wisdom, God does not immediately step in to prevent every murder of a child, every massacre, every act of injustice and exploitation. Nor does the Bible give approval to such evil.

But many Christians do not want to find out what the Bible teaches. They'd rather put the Bible in golden covers, ceremonially parade it up and down the aisle at church, and daydream while Scripture is read to them. Nor, by and large, do the ministers help them. A large percentage of mainline clergy do not believe the Bible is God's self-revelation.

4. Churchgoing

The Enemy says, "Hell is just an invention of fundamentalist preachers." Accept that, and you're two-thirds of the way to being a backslider. After all, there are plenty of things to do with a Sunday morning besides going to church. You can entertain. Play golf. Read the paper. Go for a walk.

In addition, the devil goes on, "How could a loving God seriously send anyone to hell? It's not as if you're actually *bad*. Just think of the billions of people who have rejected Jesus Christ. Do you think they're going to hell too? At least you're a member of a church. Your name is on the rolls. You go there once a year. If you end up in hell, you'll be in good company."

And so today we have countless churchgoers, with their names on the church rolls, who deny the very heart and soul of the gospel.

5. Women's ordination

The Enemy says, "God is a God of equality." Accept that, and you're two-thirds of the way to ignoring God's own principles of leadership. Nobody denies that men and women are equal in matters of salvation and in every other way. In Christ, wrote Paul, there is no Jew and no Gentile, no male and no female (Galatians 3:28). But in the area of church authority, the principle is that of different roles.

The Bible is clear; there is no room for argument. Cling blindly to the equality principle, no matter what, and you will find yourself saying that Paul hated women, that he had a Jewish preoccupation with male leadership, and that we must distinguish in the epistles between what Paul the apostle said and what Paul the Jewish rabbi said.

6. Gay rights

The Enemy says, "God doesn't condemn loving, homosexual relationships." Accept that, and you're two-thirds of the way to ignoring God's design for sex and marriage. Throughout the Bible, God clearly condemns the practice of homosexuality while praising marriage between one man and one woman. So the Enemy has been hard at work in our society, promoting homosexuality and undermining traditional marriage. Those who refuse to approve of gay marriage are called bigots.

God is clear: we must love what he loves and condemn what he condemns, no matter what society says.

But God is clear: we must love what he loves and condemn what he condemns, no matter what society says. Remember this: we all are tempted to sin. The power of the gospel is that God empowers us to overcome temptations of all kinds.

Fact 2: The Enemy Goes to Church

If you think the Enemy is going to come through the church doors and say, "Uh-uh, that's not a place for me," you are already deceived.

Satan has moved into many a church. He has introduced his own standards and gotten people to accept them. He has made his falsehood into their gospel. He has positioned his emissaries in their leadership. Someone said, "Satan is not fighting churches. He is joining them." It's true. For he does more harm by sowing tares than by pulling up wheat. He accomplishes more by infiltration than he does by frontal attack. After all, the most dangerous lie is the lie that resembles the truth. In this way the Enemy is able to use churches to pull people into his territory. These churches become fronts for his operation. They resemble real churches, live churches, but they are dead and they are staffed by false teachers. Let me tell you how they work.

The most dangerous lie is the lie that resembles the truth.

There is a selling technique called the bait-and-switch method. To entice people into a store, the retailer advertises well-known brand-name merchandise for a very low price. But when the customer comes in to purchase that brand, he is regretfully informed it is out of stock. He is then offered an alternative—an inferior brand, which nevertheless costs more money. The brand-name item used to bring the customer into the store may never have been in stock at all.

Believe me, this is how the Enemy works in churches. He sets up his phony leaders, his false teachers. They use biblical words, they use biblical terms, to capture and gain the seekers' ears. They talk about Christ, redemption, the cross, the resurrection—without believing in any of them. They do not submit to the gospel. They do not live under its authority. They use the language of truth because that is the language that draws people in. But there's no truth there, and there never was. When a seeker arrives in the church—just like the customer attracted by bait-and-switch advertising—he is confronted not with the true gospel, but with an inferior alternative, a pattern of belief and behavior contrary to the Word of God.

I have seen this in action. I once asked a West Coast minister (who is now dead), "Why do you so often use the phrase 'the risen Christ' in your sermons? Why do you keep using that expression when you have told me that you do not believe that Jesus rose from the grave?"

"Very simple," he said. "Number one, I believe that Jesus' soul is risen, just like the soul of every other dead person. But also, the few conservatives who give most of the money really like this stuff." He meant the believers. He called them conservatives.

Surprised? You shouldn't be. False teachers have been among God's people from the earliest times. What else were the Pharisees but false teachers? When Jesus came among them—Jesus the truth, the whole truth, the full embodiment of the truth of God—the Pharisees rejected him. Listen to what Jesus said to them: "You are of your father the devil, and your will is to do your father's desires"

(John 8:44). It is horrifying to think these words can be applied, no less aptly, to some church leaders today. They are false teachers, just as the Pharisees were. They preside over the same kinds of religious hierarchy. And they are taken in by the Enemy in just the same way.

The apostle Paul told Timothy: "Now the Spirit expressly says that in later times some will depart from the faith by devoting themselves to deceitful spirits and teachings of demons" (1 Timothy 4:1). As I spend time in fasting and prayer before the Lord, and as I look at the world and see what's going on, I am convinced in my own heart that Satan senses his end is near. He knows the time will soon come for his deception to be exposed and for him to be thrown into the lake of fire. And the closer we get to that time, the more he turns up the heat of deception. Christians are his primary targets. Satan is trying to take the strategic high ground in the church because from there he can divert people from the truth. Slowly, subtly, the truth of God's Word is being denied.

> I am convinced that Satan senses his end is near. And the closer we get to that time, the more he turns up the heat of deception.

Watch out. And don't make the mistake of expecting too little of your leaders, for that is also a trick of the Enemy. I have a precious brother whom I love dearly. But he worships in one of those churches that denies the gospel of Christ. He called me one day, full of excitement, and said, "Listen, good news, good news!"

"What's happening?" I asked.

"Our minister mentioned Jesus by name in the sermon yesterday. That is a positive step."

I must confess to you I did not know whether to be angry or to weep. Yet I find weeping to be much healthier than being angry, so I wept. Not only had the Enemy captured that church, he had so lowered the expectations of the congregation that even God's true believers expected nothing different.

Fact 3: The Enemy Wants to Meet Your Needs

How many times have I heard Christians in America say, "I wish I could find a church that meets my needs"?

I want to tell you that this is deception, pure and simple. There is not a soul alive today who can meet your needs. The pastor can't meet your needs. The church board can't meet your needs. The Sunday school teachers can't meet your needs. Nobody can meet your needs except the Lord Jesus Christ. And yet people go along on a Sunday morning and ask themselves, *What can I get out of church? What benefit is there for me in this? Where is the payoff?* Their attention is focused entirely on themselves.

But to have your needs met, you must first stop thinking about yourself. You must worship the living God, bow before him, honor and glorify him. You must say, "God, you are the Creator of the world, you are the Savior of my soul." Then, and only then, can your needs be met.

Nevertheless, many congregations have started to think of themselves as need-meeters. They have fallen into the Enemy's trap by asking what *they* can do as an organization to meet the needs of their members. Slowly they are starting to exclude God from the picture. They are like storekeepers who think they can satisfy the needs of their customers by showing them around the empty shelves. Ultimately the needs of those coming into a store are met by something that comes from elsewhere. The storekeeper does not sew the shirt, does not kill the cow and cut it into steaks. He simply sells the goods that somebody else puts on the shelf.

How many of us have had the experience of seeking something from a church but finding it like a store with nothing but empty shelves? For no church is perfect. You can always find fault. Maybe the children's ministry is not what you hoped it would be. Maybe the service isn't warm or lively enough for your tastes, or maybe it's too warm and too lively. As long as you are expecting something from the other *people* at the church, you are going to be disappointed, and as soon as you are disappointed you will start to poison the fellowship with your dissatisfaction.

It is no coincidence that the New Testament makes so much of the tongue. James said,

> But no human being can tame the tongue. It is a restless evil, full of deadly poison. With it we bless our Lord and Father, and with it we curse people who are made in the likeness of God (James 3:8-9).

By gossiping and spreading rumors, by maligning others, by airing our grievances, by impugning others' motives and leveling false accusations, we give our tongues to the Enemy. We let him use them to destroy the fellowship of the saints. If a church is going to collapse or split, that is often how the process begins.

Having said that, it is evident when a church loves Jesus; the members end up helping one another. That is a given for a New Testament church.

So here again, remember the questions I put to you earlier: Who do you resemble? Who do you imitate? The Enemy of your soul? Or the Lord of your life?

Fact 4: The Enemy Is a Supreme Forger

I used to think the Enemy's work would be clearly recognizable—that his methods would be unique and any territory he took would be clearly marked with his flag. I was wrong. I am not inexperienced; with the exception of one short eighteen-month period when I wandered off, I have been walking with the Lord since 1964 and have long had a gift of discernment. And yet, again and again, Satan's emissaries have sneaked up on me unawares—because the counterfeit product and the genuine article can look very much alike.

This is no accident. As we saw in the last chapter, the Enemy appears as an angel of light. His whole program is to emulate God. He wants people to think he is God. He even attempted to topple God from his throne. This failed, and God threw him out of the heavens as a result. But he continues to believe in his own divinity and continues to insist that others believe in it too. And in a sense this is logical. For in that part of creation the Enemy controls, his powers resemble God's. That is why the Bible calls him "the god of this world."

> Satan continues to believe in his own divinity and
> continues to insist that others believe in it too.

The Bible gives us some clear examples of Satan's imitation. You can see it in the story of Moses before the pharaoh:

> Then the LORD said to Moses and Aaron, "When Pharaoh says to you, 'Prove yourselves by working a miracle,' then you shall say to Aaron, 'Take your staff and cast it down before Pharaoh, that it may become a serpent.'" So Moses and Aaron went to Pharaoh and did just as the LORD commanded. Aaron cast down his staff before Pharaoh and his servants, and it became a serpent. Then Pharaoh summoned the wise men and the sorcerers, and they, the magicians of Egypt, also did the same by their secret arts. For each man cast down his staff, and they became serpents (Exodus 7:8-12).

The next sentence reads, "But Aaron's staff swallowed up their staffs." In other words, we are left in no doubt as to the shoddiness of the Enemy's workmanship. Nevertheless, we should not underestimate his ability to run a good advertising campaign. We are explicitly warned in the book of Revelation that the second beast, the beast from the land,

performs great signs, even making fire come down from
heaven to earth in front of people, and by the signs
that it is allowed to work in the presence of the beast it
deceives those who dwell on earth, telling them to make
an image for the beast that was wounded by the sword
and yet lived (Revelation 13:13-14).

So if you are one of those Christians who runs around looking
for miracles, be very careful. Miracles can be phony. People claiming to work miracles are a dime a dozen, and just because a miracle worker is standing in a pulpit does not guarantee that he is on
God's side.

Don't ever forget: The devil is a preacher.
He is diabolical in his preaching, but
he is a preacher nonetheless.

Don't ever forget: The devil is a preacher. He is diabolical in his
preaching, but he is a preacher nonetheless. He preaches another
gospel, he preaches another Jesus, he preaches another power. And
all of his demons have the same ability. They are all licensed and
have credentials to preach. They will even concede a few periph-
eral doctrines in order to win your assent in denying the heart of
the faith. They will cheerfully talk for hours on the importance of
behaving in a godly manner, so long as they are not required to say
that salvation comes only through the shed blood of Christ. That
is the line they will never cross, because it is, in effect, the front line,
the line dividing the forces of the Enemy from the forces of God.

In Acts, Elymas the sorcerer refused to cross that line. You will
remember from Acts 13 that Barnabas and Paul had been preaching
to Sergius Paulus, the proconsul of Paphos on the island of Cyprus.

But Elymas the magician (for that is the meaning of his
name) opposed them, seeking to turn the proconsul away

> from the faith. But Saul, who was also called Paul, filled
> with the Holy Spirit, looked intently at him and said,
> "You son of the devil, you enemy of all righteousness,
> full of all deceit and villainy, will you not stop making
> crooked the straight paths of the Lord?" (Acts 13:8-10).

The grounds of the conflict are clear. Luke, the writer of Acts, has already said that the proconsul "summoned Barnabas and Saul and sought to hear the word of God" (v. 7). Elymas tried to turn this man "away from the faith." He did not do it out of misplaced good-will or by accident. Paul saw straight to the heart of the issue when he denounced Elymas: "You son of the devil, you enemy of all righteousness, full of all deceit and villainy, will you not stop making crooked the straight paths of the Lord?"

That insight, we are told, came straight from the Holy Spirit. It was Paul's gift of discernment. He could see through the imitation. He could distinguish the brand name from the cheap imitation, the copy from the genuine article. It is a gift the Enemy prefers us not to have, but one we need badly.

Fact 5: The Enemy Detests the Down-and-Out

Once I was walking downtown with a Christian brother. We passed a wino sitting in a doorway. The knees of his pants were worn through, and the soles were working loose from his shoes. My companion heaved a sigh and remarked, "Look at him. Don't you think that's Satan's masterpiece?"

I disagreed. The man was in a bad way, to be sure. He was to be pitied, to be reached out to. But it is a gross mistake to think that the Enemy takes any special pride in a piece of work like that. Far more likely, he reacts to a wino with disgust and nausea. Why would someone who thinks he is God want to surround himself with derelicts from skid row? Satan may well think himself a great artist when it comes to molding human destinies, but to find his masterpieces you will have to look someplace other than the gutter.

Satan's masterpiece is someone who is upstanding, someone who is respectable, someone who is a community leader, *but who feels that he or she does not need Jesus Christ.*

Satan's masterpiece is someone who commands admiration, who is successful, who is strong and independent to the point of ignoring the claims of Christ.

Satan's masterpiece is the media personality who uses all the glamour of his or her position to tell us that true goodness means promoting gay rights and taking a prochoice stance.

Satan's masterpiece is a bishop in the church who says, "The Bible is an archaic book. God will never judge anybody. Live any way you like."

You see, when Satan appears as an angel of light, it means he wants his followers to appear kind, gentle, and accommodating, to be into diversity, pluralism, and political correctness. More than anything else, to be *tolerant.* Note, however, that being tolerant generally *includes* all forms of sexual perversion but *excludes* godly living after the pattern of Scripture. Hence the outcry against prayer in Jesus' name at public events.

Note also how the good work of Christian believers is ignored or taken for granted, while the media gives extensive coverage to the movie stars' charitable balls and concerts. Every day, those who believe in the Lord Jesus Christ give themselves to others in selfless service. And yet this goes almost completely unacknowledged, while the crumbs that fall from the tables of the godless rich are greeted with fanfares, as though Hollywood alone could take credit for the world's salvation.

It is ironic that the philosophies espoused by followers of the Enemy—the philosophies of evolution and political correctness—are so woefully inadequate. They say, in effect, that men and women can make it on their own, that human perfection is attainable without the help of God. But what is happening as these philosophies tighten their grip on America?

Turn on your television and you will see that the sociologists and other experts are baffled by the growth of violence, the rise in crime, the erosion of standards. All they can do is recommend throwing more money at social problems. Raise budgets. Put more police on the streets. Pass more laws. Strengthen government. Set higher educational standards. None of which can do more than tinker with the problem, because their analysis of the problem is wrong. Their underlying assumptions are wrong. Humankind is not perfectible without the intervention of God. The answer to social problems is not to keep God out of public life; it is to let God back in.

But no. The Enemy now dominates the secular media. He wants to make his followers believe the lie that they can be perfect without having a relationship with Jesus Christ. In doing so he readily makes use of Christian values—compassion, care, understanding—because these provide him with an ideal cover. After all, who would join his side if he was known to be planning the total ruin of those who serve him?

He did not tell Eve that eating the fruit would get her thrown out of Eden. He pointed only to the fruit's advantages. It is in the Enemy's interests, therefore, to maintain the illusion that serving him is lucrative, that everyone has something to gain.

> Satan's best work is to be found among beautiful people who are seeking to be perfect without Jesus.

Don't ever fall into the temptation of thinking that Satan is in the ghettos and the gutters. He assigns his most incompetent demons to those cases. His best work is to be found in the upper echelons, among beautiful people who are seeking to be perfect without Jesus. He is most often to be found with those who, like him, prefer to think themselves gods.

Fact 6: The Enemy Disguises Falsehood with Truth

Some time ago I read a story about a British art critic named Devine. Devine took his daughter to the ocean one day for a picnic, but he could not persuade the little girl to go with him into the chilly Atlantic waters. So he built a fire on the beach and heated some water in a teakettle. When it had boiled, he picked up the teakettle and with great ceremony poured the hot steamy water into the ocean.

"Now it's warm, and you can go in," he told his daughter.

The little girl saw not an ocean full of cold water but the kettle-ful of hot water. And she ran gleefully in.

The story illustrates how the Enemy tempts us. He sprinkles the ocean of falsehood with a tiny drop of truth. But he does it with such a flourish, people see only the truth and not the falsehood— and so wade into it by the millions, not realizing they have been deceived.

The Enemy sprinkles the ocean of
falsehood with a tiny drop of truth.

Let me give you some examples of how the Enemy can use truth to deceive you.

1. In business

Say you're a businessman or a businesswoman who is a Christian, and you want to operate your business according to biblical principles. The Enemy comes in and says, "Good, good. Biblical principles are wonderful. They deserve our respect, and there is no doubt that in the past they have worked for all sorts of people."

That's all true. But then he goes on, "Don't forget, though, that these are modern times. Things are different now. Everyone is a little closer to that bottom line. You have less room to maneuver. So if the competition cuts corners, you have to do the same. Blindly sticking up for principles will put you out of business. And God doesn't want you to be out of business, does he? He wants to bless you."

It's the old argument that the end justifies the means. But it seems compelling. For what does a businessperson fear more than insolvency? And how many good causes—family, employee security, philanthropies—can a Christian businessperson point to that will suffer if the business slides?

2. In personal life

Everybody has problems. If you are a Christian, you will take your problems to the Lord and seek his power and his wisdom to show you the way forward. But problems are seldom resolved with a snap of the fingers, and in the meantime you find yourself fighting uncertainty and discouragement and anxiety. Then the Enemy whispers in your ear: "Things getting tough? Need to forget your troubles for a while? Then have a drink."

No sooner have you rejected this idea than the Enemy comes back at you. "Remember, drinking is biblical." Biblical? "Ever read Paul's first epistle to Timothy?" he says. "'No longer drink only water, but use a little wine for the sake of your stomach and your frequent ailments.' Read it yourself. It's right there in 1 Timothy 5:23. If the apostle Paul allowed drinking, surely it's okay."

Here again, the Enemy is using truth. Paul *did* urge Timothy to drink a little wine. But there the truth ends, for a sip of wine taken for medicinal purposes is not the same thing as drinking a couple of double scotches because life is getting on top of you. Don't be surprised if the Enemy quotes Scripture to you. After all, he quoted Scripture to Jesus during the temptation in the wilderness. And the Enemy knows his Scriptures well.

3. In dating

Imagine a single person who has prayed fervently to God for a spouse, but whose prayers seem not to have been heard. The Enemy sympathizes. "God hasn't answered your prayer?" he says. "That's too bad."

All true. And then he moves on from the truth to something else. "Maybe you're not understanding God right. Maybe what he really wants you to do is to date an unbeliever. That way you get a date, and God gets a new convert. Anyway, dating is not the same as getting married. You don't have to talk about marriage. Just enjoy the dating."

I have met a lot of people who have taken this advice and bitterly regretted it. After all, we are not in control enough of our emotions to stop dating from turning into something more permanent. And being married to the wrong person is worse than not being married at all.

4. In tithing

The Bible is absolutely clear about tithing. Tithing is like a tax. Would you dodge the IRS? Of course not. But countless Christians dodge God. They do not give anything near a tenth of their income to God's work. They listen to the Enemy, who whispers in their ears, "You know, God really doesn't need your money. After all, doesn't the Bible say he owns the cattle on a thousand hills?" Quite right. It does say that. But it also tells us to tithe.

"Ah," the Enemy goes on, "but what about all those other God-given responsibilities you have? You must be prudent with your money. You need to have this particular house, you must have this particular car, you must have things for the kitchen and things for the dining room and things for the living room. Do you want to raise your kids without giving them all the material advantages their friends enjoy?"

That one hits hard, doesn't it? I took my daughter to college some time ago, along with all the other parents. We were all unloading stuff: books, files, boxes, suitcases, clothes, pictures, stereos, CDs, computers. Every one of us seemed to have packed half a house in the back of the car. We lugged it all upstairs to our children's rooms—rooms so small that it was a struggle to get everything in. On about the second or third journey up the stairs, it struck me that we are a nation of things. We can't get along without things: things we really don't need but can't bear to be without. And it's a problem for the parents as much as for the children.

"After all," the Enemy continues, "you've got the future to think about. Pensions. Insurance. The mortgage. Holidays. God knows you can't cover all that *and* pay him 10 percent. Just put a couple of dollars in the plate when it comes around on Sunday morning, to show that you're doing your bit. Put a ten-dollar bill in if you want to look generous. But don't use the money you need for other things."

> God does not need our gifts. He does
> not ask us to give for *his* sake at all. He
> asks us to give for *our* sakes.

Of course this is a miser's philosophy. Give as little as you can to others, and save as much as you can for yourself. But what does the Bible tell us? It tells us we have turned the truth on its head. Certainly God does not need our gifts. He does not ask us to give for *his* sake at all. He asks us to give for *our* sakes. If we develop a giving, Christ-centered heart, if we learn to stretch the dollars we spend on ourselves so we have dollars left to give away, we will be blessed. It is that blessing the Enemy is so anxious to deprive you of—a blessing that will come not just financially but in ways you have not even dreamed of. Just read the prophet Malachi:

> "Bring the full tithe into the storehouse, that there may
> be food in my house. And thereby put me to the test,
> says the Lord of hosts, if I will not open the windows of
> heaven for you and pour down for you a blessing until
> there is no more need" (Malachi 3:10).

Fact 7: The Enemy Never Attacks from the Front

There are some sins that every believer condemns. These are what might be called the big moral sins: unfaithfulness, unchasteness, dishonesty, false belief. The big moral sins have an immediate impact because everyone agrees they are wrong and in most cases they are very clear-cut. Do you remember what happened not long ago when some Christian leaders were disgraced because of secret adulteries and underhanded financial dealings? Once those sins were out in the open, nobody could defend them. Nobody wanted to.

But there are other sins that never make the headlines. I call them the *socially acceptable sins.* They are socially acceptable because most of them are so widespread, Christians have covered them with a conspiracy of silence. And yet the socially acceptable sins have the greatest long-range negative impact upon you, your family, and the body of Christ. They are sins that express conflict in our ordinary day-to-day relationships at home and at church. Sins that happen between husband and wife, children and parents, colleague and colleague, church member and church member. Sins like:

- gossiping and murmuring
- a critical spirit
- an unforgiving heart
- rebellion against God's principles in marriage and home
- a husband's abdication of spiritual responsibility in the home
- a wife's resentment of her husband's spiritual leadership
- a child's refusal to obey parents
- a desire for self-promotion
- putting others down
- spiritual pride and jealousy
- divisiveness and rebellion against spiritual authority

For example, you may think you are having a prayer meeting. But listen to what is being said in and around the prayer. Are you really praying together, or are you getting together to gossip and complain? You may think you are having a counseling session. But listen to what is being discussed. Is it any more than an airing of resentments and bitterness? And what about that sermon? Were you hearing God's truth proclaimed from the pulpit, or was this really an exercise in self-promotion and spiritual pride?

Because of these socially acceptable sins, situations in which believers ought to be coming closer together in the Spirit instead become points of friction and disharmony.

Listen carefully to the words of Jesus. In the hours before his trial and crucifixion, he prayed one of the most significant prayers recorded in the New Testament. He prayed to his Father for all his disciples, those already living and those yet to be born:

> "I do not ask for these only, but also for those who will believe in me through their word, that they may all be one, just as you, Father, are in me, and I in you, that they also may be in us, so that the world may believe that you have sent me. The glory that you have given me I have given to them, that they may be one even as we are one, I in them and you in me, that they may become perfectly one, so that the world may know that you sent me and loved them even as you loved me" (John 17:20-23).

The phrase "that they may all be one" or "that they may become perfectly one" occurs three times in this passage. Jesus was asking that believers be *one* together and that believers be *one* with God. For only in that oneness will the world see as well as hear the gospel. The unity of believers is the greatest demonstration of the love of God. That unity, that oneness, is what will bring sinners to Christ. Not just preaching, though the Word must be preached if it is to be believed, but living out the Word in the unity of the church.

> The unity of believers is the greatest
> demonstration of the love of God. That unity, that
> oneness, is what will bring sinners to Christ.

Now if you are ever tempted to think Satan is stupid, think again. Satan is not stupid. He knows exactly how to counter the evangelization of the world. He knows because he has studied the Bible very carefully—more carefully than many Christians have. He knows that to stifle the spread of the gospel, one of his main objectives must be to undermine the unity of Christians. So he does everything in his power to accomplish that. Whenever husband and wife have an argument and go to bed without forgiving each other (or at least resolving to deal with the issue), Satan has succeeded. Whenever two believers in Jesus Christ are in ongoing conflict with each other, Satan has succeeded.

Yet if the Enemy relied only on frontal assault, if he came in his true colors, discerning believers would get together on their knees before God and start praying. And God would give them victory. But the Enemy is too crafty to use a frontal assault.

Let me tell you a helpful story I heard during my boyhood in Egypt.

It is said that in the fifth century a famous holy man used to spend much time at prayer in the desert, just as Jesus did. Like Jesus, this holy man suffered temptations. So righteous was he that the devil sent a whole posse of demons on a special assignment to entice and trip him—to do whatever it took to make this man of God fall. They used all the usual methods. Lustful thoughts to drag down his spirit. Fatigue to keep him from prayer. Hunger to make him abandon his fasts. But no matter what they tried, or how hard they worked, again and again their efforts came to nothing. In the end Satan was so annoyed at the incompetence of his minions, he pulled them off the project and took over himself.

"The reason you have failed," he lectured them, "is that you used methods too crude for such a man. He will not fall to a direct assault. You must be subtle and take him by surprise. Now watch the master at work!"

The devil then approached the holy man of God, and very softly whispered these words into his ear: "Your brother has been made the bishop of Alexandria."

Instantly the holy man's jaw stiffened. His eyes narrowed. His nostrils flared. Bishop of Alexandria? His brother? What an outrage!

Now this is a legend, not history. But it makes an important point. Notice that the demons who tempted the holy man got nowhere by using the big moral sins. He could see them coming a mile off and could defend himself. So what did Satan do? He used a socially acceptable sin. He even tailored it to the man's particular weakness. He knew that this man was guarding against the temptations of the flesh, and that it was futile to try to ambush him that way. So he sneaked up using envy and spiritual pride. He made him think, *Hey, I'm the godly one in the family. Why is my brother getting to be the bishop of Alexandria and not me?*

So watch out for the socially acceptable sins. Satan knows that if he comes out in the open and fights a biblically sound, Christ-loving church, he will lose. So he will not even try. Instead he will attack from another direction. He will infiltrate the churches with people who have spiritual pride, people who are possessed with critical spirits, people who are seeking self-promotion, people who cannot distinguish between a true angel of light and the fallen angel masquerading as an angel of light. And through them he will begin to sow the seed of doubt. He will begin to sow the seed of discontent. He will begin to sow the seed of division and partisan spirit. And before you know it, the church's leadership will be running around trying to put fires out and losing their fire for God and the gospel.

One of the Enemy's most potent tactics is to *divide and rule*. His pattern in the church is to divide and rule, divide and rule. There were times at the general council of my father's denomination in Egypt that I wondered whether this was a general synod or a Mafia meeting, so vehemently did the delegates shout and denounce one another. I thought perhaps it had something to do with Middle Eastern culture. But when I moved to Australia, where I lived and ministered for eight years, I found Christians there fighting just as hard—only more politely.

> Satan wants us to stop fighting as soldiers
> of the cross and begin fighting each
> other as soldiers of our own opinions.

Satan wants us to stop fighting as soldiers of the cross and begin fighting each other as soldiers of our own opinions. For then the war turns inward, and we begin to destroy one another instead of fighting our real Enemy.

THE ENEMY IS WORKING IN THE CHURCH

Take a look at some of the deceptions Satan has succeeded in disseminating in many a church, stripping its members of the power of the gospel.

Pornography

Pornography is one of Satan's most insidious weapons. It is a sin that is addictive, yet it is easy to hide. Many Christians feel awkward mentioning pornography. "This is not an issue for polite company," they might say. But Satan uses our discomfort to his advantage. He wants Christians to keep this issue obscured. Why? Because pornography can destroy your character, your marriage, and your church.

Just how big is the problem? The pornography industry is pervasive. It is estimated that 12 percent of all websites are pornographic. That's over twenty-four million websites. Forty million Americans regularly visit pornographic websites and 70 percent of men between the ages of eighteen and twenty-four visit pornographic sites at least once a month.[1] The industry is valued at $13 billion, more than the revenue of Microsoft, Google, Amazon, eBay, Yahoo, Apple, Netflix, and EarthLink combined.[2]

The Enemy uses this huge industry to corrupt both adults and children. Nine out of ten boys are exposed to pornography before the age of eighteen, with the average age being eleven.[3] Satan wants your children to have a distorted view of sexuality. He knows Proverbs 22:6:

> Train up a child in the way he should go;
> even when he is old he will not depart from it.

If the Enemy can get your children to have a distorted view of sexuality from an early age, he knows they will suffer from it for years to come.

The Enemy wants us to believe that pornography is mostly harmless. That is far from the truth. Here are several reasons why pornography is harmful, even deadly:

- It commercializes sexuality, teaching people (men in particular) to view sex as a monetary transaction rather than a deeply spiritual act designed only for marriage.

- It distorts our brains. Scientific studies have shown that pornography is not a neutral experience.[4] It literally rewires the brain. Pornography creates neural pathways in the brain that make men view all women as potential porn stars.[5] Where God wants men to treat women with holiness and purity, as if they were sisters, Satan uses pornography to turn women into sexual objects and ruin Christian fellowship.

- It creates false expectations of intimacy between men and women, since what is shown on a screen cannot be replicated in a marriage.

- It destroys your moral character. Research has shown
  that regularly watching pornography causes you to be
  sympathetic to adultery and same-sex marriage.[6] The
  Enemy uses this sin to desensitize us to other family and
  societal evils. Pornography leads to the breakdown of
  both the family and the church.

All this can be discouraging. But God's Word gives us insight on
how to fight sexual immorality—and the hope to prevail over it. In
a moment I will provide you some specific instructions from the
apostle Paul that helped a church facing similar issues. But first let
me give you a general overview of what the Bible has to say about
pornography.

The term *pornography* comes from the Greek word *porneia*,
which is used over twenty-five times in the New Testament. It refers
to any illicit sexual intercourse, such as adultery, fornication, and
homosexuality, and the production and use of pornography would
certainly fall into this category.[7] Jesus uses the term *porneia* in several places, and in Matthew 15:19 he condemns it along with evil
thoughts, murder, adultery, theft, lying, and blasphemy.

The apostle Paul uses *porneia* six times in his letters to the Corinthians. The church at Corinth struggled a great deal with con-
formity to the Greek and Roman world, which was full of sexual
immorality. Here is how Paul told the Christians at Corinth to fight
against rampant sexual immorality:

> Flee from sexual immorality. Every other sin a person
> commits is outside the body, but the sexually immoral
> person sins against his own body (1 Corinthians 6:18).

Here is Paul's instruction: Flee! The Greek word here is *pheugo*,
which means to "flee (to shun or avoid by flight) something abhor-
rent, especially vices." Another definition is "to be saved by flight, to
escape safely out of danger."[8] Paul is telling us that sexual immorality

is unlike any other sin. It is so dangerous that our only option is to physically run from it.

So how do we flee from pornography? Even if you do not struggle with pornography, you should consider setting up filters and meeting with an accountability partner who receives a list of all the websites you visit every month. Just as the Enemy uses technology to disseminate pornography, Christians should use technology to protect themselves from the poisonous effects of pornography. Don't ever put yourself in a position where you can have easy, hidden access to pornography. The temptation is too great and the consequences too severe.

Universalism

Universalism is the belief that God will save everyone in the whole world.

Yes, everyone.

It only takes a moment to realize the error of this view. It trivializes evil and mocks justice. In universalism, even murderous dictators get to go to heaven. It doesn't matter what you do on this earth, since God will save you in the end. Why then are these persecuted Christians dying for their faith?

Why do evangelism? Why even try to reach the "lost," since they will be saved anyway? Universalism is a grave error that makes a mockery of the cross and gives unbelievers false hope.

Insider Movement

The insider movement teaches that a Muslim who is converted to Christ can remain a Muslim, call himself a Muslim, recite Islamic prayers in the mosque, say that there is no god but Allah, and as long as he believes in Jesus, he is a Christian.

This is one of the most dangerous movements in our time. Just as universalism destroyed the mainline denominations, this insider movement has the potential to destroy many evangelical churches.

> The insider movement is one of the most
> dangerous teachings in our time.

This dangerous teaching is nothing short of the old syncretism that brought Israel down.

Respecting local customs and local culture, and even the effort to contextualize the gospel as so many others have done successfully, is all well and good. But out and out heretical teaching, such as claiming that Muhammad is a prophet and that converts from Islam need not turn their backs on this antibiblical religion, is nothing short of a denial of the heart of the gospel.

There is a great difference between following local customs and becoming so much like the local culture that you are no longer a professing Christian. Paul never sacrificed his Christian beliefs for cultural ones. Christians are called to distinguish themselves from the world around them, especially in their behavior (Romans 12:2; Ephesians 2:1-10). Since Islam preaches a false gospel, how can a faithful Christian regularly attend mosque and pray Muslim prayers?

Hyper-Grace

The hyper-grace movement (sometimes called modern grace) claims to have a new and liberating understanding of the gospel, one that was missed by Luther and Calvin during the Protestant Reformation. Those who follow hyper-grace want to say that their movement is all about *grace*. What could be wrong with that? Isn't grace biblical?

Hyper-grace adherents think you should never call Christians to live a life of holiness. If a Christian is saved, they say, that person is completely perfected in God already. There is no need to worry about sin or asking God for forgiveness.

The problem is not that these people believe in grace, but that they do not take grace seriously enough. If we appreciate God's grace, should we not obey him out of gratitude? And God repeatedly calls us to pursue holiness (Romans 6:19; 2 Corinthians 7:1; 1 Thessalonians 4:7; Hebrews 12:14). Anyone who claims we do not need to actively work toward righteous behavior in our lives is not honoring the Lord.

Charles Spurgeon is said to have constantly repeated a statement that goes something like this: "The grace that does not lead to holy living is not God's grace."

We must remain ever vigilant against these and other deceptions that Satan is intent on using to undermine the body of Christ, stripping its members of the power of the gospel. As believers, we must instead fill our minds with the truths of God's Word and model our lives on those truths.

CHAPTER 3

THE ENEMY'S CHAIN
OF COMMAND

ack in the seventies, John Vaughan, formerly of the Mega-
church Research Center and Southwest Baptist University in
Bolivar, Missouri, was on a flight from Detroit to Boston.
He had not paid much attention to the man in the next seat, but
noticed after a while that the man had bowed his head and was moving his lips as if praying. When he finished, Vaughan said, "Are you
a Christian?"

The man seemed shocked. "Oh, no," he said. "You have me all
wrong. I'm not a Christian. I'm a satanist."

Curious, Vaughan asked what he had been praying for.

"Do you really want to know?"

Vaughan assured him that he did, and the man told him. "My
primary attention is directed toward the fall of Christian pastors and
their families living in New England." He paused. "And what's your
business in Boston?" he asked Vaughan.

"I'm editor of the *Journal of the American Society for Church
Growth*. I'm going to Boston to do a pastors' seminar."

Vaughan outlined his ministry and its purposes for the kingdom of God, and shortly afterward the satanist indicated that he needed to return to his work!

Does that story alarm you? It should. C. Peter Wagner, who records this encounter in his book *Prayer Shield*, documents how all over the North American continent satanists were gathering for the specific purpose of praying against evangelical Christian leaders. They concentrated on key pastors across the land and targeted them for failure. They had networks of prayer to Satan, each one taking responsibility for a particular region. They prayed for the families of leading evangelicals to break up.

Why *leading* evangelicals? The answer has to be that the Enemy knows the importance of a command structure. We are not just using descriptive language when we talk about the church as an army and Christians as soldiers of Christ. The church is indeed a fighting organization. It follows a battle plan and needs strong, insightful leaders to coordinate its campaigns. Satan knows full well that when a pastor falls, the ripples spread far and wide through the Christian community. If a solitary man sins, he alone suffers the consequences.

Much better, then, from the Enemy's point of view, to go for a person of influence—the family man, the community leader, the national politician. For the corruption of such an individual melts down through his whole field of influence. The wider that field of influence is, the greater the damage caused by the sin. Who can forget Adolf Hitler, who not only ruined Germany but flooded almost the whole continent of Europe with the misery of Nazi repression?

The Enemy understands command structures because he himself operates one. The demonic hierarchy, in fact, closely shadows its angelic counterpart. Satan too is fighting a war. He too has his generals and his field commanders. He too maintains order and discipline to assist his twin aims of harassing Christians and keeping the unsaved spiritually blind. His forces are rebels who have broken away from God's angelic army, taking with them not only their weapons but also their ranks and divisions.

> In organizing his demon hordes, Satan has not
> created anything new, for he is incapable of
> creating. He has only stolen ideas from elsewhere.

Satan is a copycat. He has copied the angelic order. In organizing his demon hordes, he has not created anything new, for he is incapable of creating. He has only stolen ideas from elsewhere. In this way, Satan and political liberals have something in common. The liberals in this country never establish great institutions. They never start great schools. They only hijack them from the godly men and women who founded them. That is the Enemy's way. But ironically, it has one advantage for us. If we want to understand the Enemy's organization, we can find no better way to start than examining the genuine article: the hierarchy of angels from which Satan broke away.

THE HEAVENLY HOST

We use the term *angel* frivolously. We say to someone, "Oh, you are an angel." We tend to say it most often to women, little girls, and babies. And we usually say it when they have done something that pleases us. I have yet to hear a parent call a child an angel when he is screaming his head off or throwing food at the dinner table. At such times parents use other words, but not *angel*.

> Angels are not effeminate harpists dressed
> in bed linen: They are God's marines.

From this you might suppose that angels are female, fragile, relatively weak, and concerned mainly with doing minor good works. This certainly is the way they are portrayed in many books and films. Somehow we have gotten into the habit of imagining angels with halos and wings—an image supplied not by the Bible but by old religious paintings and Christmas cards.

Most believers do not understand the nature of angels. They do not understand the activities of angels. They do not understand the form of their existence. They do not understand the purpose of the angelic realm. Most, in fact, know so little about real angels that meeting one would give them a heart attack. Why else would the angel announcing Jesus' birth to the shepherds have begun by saying, "Fear not" (Luke 2:10)? The truth is, angels are not effeminate harpists dressed in bed linen: They are God's marines.

Five Things You Need to Know About Angels

1. Angels have individual personalities.

Since the *Star Wars* films we have become familiar with the New Age idea that good exists in the universe as a nebulous supernatural force. But this is far from the truth. The heavenly host is not impersonal, nor is it a single entity. Each angel is an individual person with an individual job to do. Remember how the Christmas story begins: "In the sixth month the angel Gabriel was sent from God to a city of Galilee named Nazareth" (Luke 1:26).

Not *an angel* but *the angel Gabriel.* This angel had a name and a mission. Explaining the actions of God seems to be Gabriel's specialty, in fact, since we know he was also sent to talk to Daniel. Daniel said, "And I heard a man's voice between the banks of the Ulai, and it called, 'Gabriel, make this man understand the vision'" (Daniel 8:16).

From the Word of God we know that angels possess personality, intellect, feeling, and free will. They have different functions, but their primary responsibility is to administer the will of God, to execute the plan of God in our lives as we submit to the lordship of Jesus Christ.

2. Angels never die.

Every angel God ever created is alive today. Gabriel's appearances to Daniel and Mary, separated by hundreds of years, indicate that angels are not bound by human time spans. Also, Jesus told us that angels live according to different physical laws. Answering the Sadducees' question about divorce, he said, "For in the resurrection they neither marry nor are given in marriage, but are like angels in heaven" (Matthew 22:30).

He did not mean that men and women *become* angels—that lame idea comes from watching too many sentimental television dramas. But we become *like* angels in that we enter a realm where death does not exist. Because the angelic ranks are not depleted by death, there is no need for a system of marriage and reproduction to keep their number constant.

3. Angels have bodies.

Wherever they turn up in the Bible, angels have a physical form. "And behold, there stood before me one having the appearance of a man," Daniel said of Gabriel (Daniel 8:15). That word *appearance* is important. The celestial body is not like ours. It is a different kind of body, designed for a different kind of realm, working according to different rules. But, like our own, it has form and likeness and weight. Yet it is capable of much more.

We see Jesus clothed in such a body after his resurrection. Though Jesus reassured his disciples that he was not a disembodied spirit, it is clear he did not need to unlock the door to get into the room where they had gathered. In Luke's words,

> As they were talking about these things, Jesus himself stood among them, and said to them, "Peace to you!" But they were startled and frightened and thought they saw a spirit. And he said to them, "Why are you troubled, and why do doubts arise in your hearts? See my hands and my feet, that it is I myself. Touch me, and see. For a spirit does not have flesh and bones as you see that I have" (Luke 24:36-39).

Celestial bodies can also travel great distances at high speed. Daniel says, "while I was speaking in prayer, the man Gabriel, whom I had seen in the vision at the first, came to me in swift flight at the time of the evening sacrifice" (Daniel 9:21).

We see the same with the resurrected Jesus. One moment he was in Galilee, the next moment in Jerusalem. One moment he was talking to Mary outside the tomb, the next he was going to see his Father before returning to the Upper Room. The facts here are stranger and more wonderful than any fantasy put out by Hollywood. And while we're on the subject, don't fall for all that *Ghostbusters* nonsense about blasting evil spirits with bolts of electricity. The celestial body is indestructible.

Angels even *look* different from people. Sometimes the difference is minimal, which is why Daniel described his visiting angel as the "man Gabriel." Usually, though, an angel will be an awesome sight. Daniel described another angel in this way:

> "His body was like beryl, his face like the appearance of lightning, his eyes like flaming torches, his arms and legs like the gleam of burnished bronze, and the sound of his words like the sound of a multitude" (Daniel 10:6).

So terrifying was this angel that his presence affected even those who had not seen him.

> "And I, Daniel, alone saw the vision, for the men who were with me did not see the vision, but a great trembling fell upon them, and they fled to hide themselves. So I was left alone and saw this great vision, and no strength was left in me" (Daniel 10:7-8).

In one of his novels, C.S. Lewis pictures a visiting angel as a shaft of brilliant light so straight that it makes everything else in the room look curved. Be cautious of anyone who speaks lightly of meeting angels. If you meet an angel, you will *never* forget it.

4. Angels have different ranks.

When God began his work of creation, he did not start with the earth. He started with the angelic realm.

When God began his work of creation, he did not start with the earth. He started with the angelic realm.

Genesis says, "In the beginning God created the heavens and the earth" (1:1). Writing to the Colossians about Christ's role in creation, Paul the apostle used the same ordering: heavens first, earth second:

> For by Him all things were created that are in heaven and that are on earth, visible and invisible, whether thrones or dominions or principalities or powers. All things were created through Him and for Him (Colossians 1:16 NKJV).

Incidentally, a lot of those people who say, "What I cannot see does not exist," are going to have egg on their faces when God finally unveils the invisible world and everyone can see it.

But notice the four terms Paul used here to define the angelic hierarchy: *thrones, dominions, principalities,* and *powers.* Remember those four words, because I will come back to them again and again. Paul placed the ranks in descending order of seniority: *thrones, dominions, principalities,* and *powers.*

The powers occupy the lowest level. They are the foot soldiers, the ones sent to execute the purposes of God. Above them the angelic hierarchy sits like a pyramid, each level exercising a wider sphere of influence than the one below it. At the top is God, who executes his will and supervises the administration of his universe through the ranks of his angels. That is why the Old Testament so often refers to God as the Lord of hosts. He is the Commander in Chief of countless angelic battalions. At his word, the whole army moves. At his command, vast numbers of angelic beings obey.

Clearly God is a God of order. He is a God of rank. God does not work on the principle of equality, with the leader being only first among equals. He uses a chain of command. He loves order, and when things get *out of order,* you can be sure Satan is responsible.

In its structure the angelic hierarchy is similar to a corporation. If you work in a big company you may want to bear that in mind. The next time you are tempted to complain about your boss, or your boss's boss, or your boss's boss's boss—just remember that God has placed you there. Just as important, remember that God has placed *them* there. Your task is to serve the living God. The company may pay your salary, but you offer your labor as unto the Lord.

5. Angels have specific jobs.

In another way, however, the angelic hierarchy is very *unlike* a corporation. In many corporations, particularly at the lower levels, people tend to lose their individuality because they are all doing much the same thing. They become instruments in the production process. But not only are no two angels the same, no two angels' *jobs* are the same. Each angel God sends out has a distinctive role in the mission to protect, preserve, and take care of his elect.

> One of the most crucial jobs angels do is to frustrate the Enemy's campaign to depopulate heaven.

One of the most crucial jobs angels do is to frustrate the Enemy's campaign to depopulate heaven. If it were all up to Satan, he would prevent every man and woman on earth from coming to the saving knowledge of the Lord Jesus Christ. And whenever someone slips through the net—whenever someone accepts Christ as Savior and begins to live the Spirit-led life—Satan tries his hardest to ensure this person remains ignorant both about Satan and about the Word of God.

Ignorance is a powerful weapon in Satan's armory. God's angels, then, often do the work of bodyguards, fighting off attacks and keeping channels of communication open. Every day, unseen spiritual battles are being fought over your head.

> "For he will command his angels concerning you
>   to guard you in all your ways.
> On their hands they will bear you up,
>   lest you strike your foot against a stone."
>   (Psalm 91:11-12)

Isn't that exciting? I was born a nobody, and yet God had a plan for me. He assigned his angels to look after me. They countered my foolishness when I thought I could reach God my own way. They countered my ignorance. They steered me around the traps the Enemy had laid to prevent my coming to know the Lord Jesus Christ as Master of my life. And after that, the angels continued to watch over me day and night.

I don't know about you, but that thought thrills me, especially when I get behind the wheel of my car. I don't often preach on bad driving—it's too convicting—but a few years ago I took two of my colleagues in the car with me to make a pastoral visit. They later told me they had actually seen my angels at work!

Do you know that hundreds of miracles are
happening around you every single day,
and you're not even aware of them?

God uses angels to perform miracles in your life. Do you know that hundreds of miracles are happening around you every single day, and you're not even aware of them? God has commissioned his angels and said, "Go down. Take care of her. This is my daughter. Take care of him. This is my son." Look carefully at the Bible and you will find angels popping up in all kinds of places, fulfilling a mission to protect God's children.

Shortly after the Holy Spirit came on the church, the apostles were imprisoned by the Sadducees.

> But during the night an angel of the Lord opened the prison doors and brought them out, and said, "Go and stand in the temple and speak to the people all the words of this Life." And when they heard this, they entered the temple at daybreak and began to teach (Acts 5:19-21).

Later on, Peter was imprisoned by Herod and kept under guard, chained between two soldiers.

> And behold, an angel of the Lord stood next to him, and a light shone in the cell. He struck Peter on the side and woke him, saying, "Get up quickly." And the chains fell off his hands. And the angel said to him, "Dress yourself and put on your sandals." And he did so. And he said to him, "Wrap your cloak around you and follow me." And he went out and followed him. He did not know that what was being done by the angel was real, but thought he was seeing a vision (Acts 12:7-8).

Later, when the angel had completed his assignment by escorting Peter to the nearest intersection, he disappeared.

> When Peter came to himself, he said, "Now I am sure that the Lord has sent his angel and rescued me from the hand of Herod" (Acts 12:11).

So much for angels. What about Satan and his army?

THE INFERNAL HIERARCHY

We saw earlier that when Lucifer's pride got the better of him and he rebelled against God, he was thrown out. The attempted coup failed. Or did it? That's not the only way of looking at it. Satan may not have toppled God, but on the face of it he significantly altered the balance of power in heaven. The day after the battle, no less than a third of God's angels went AWOL and transferred their allegiance. John referred to this event in picturesque language when he wrote:

> And another sign appeared in heaven: behold, a great red dragon, with seven heads and ten horns, and on his heads seven diadems. His tail swept down a third of the stars of heaven and cast them to the earth (Revelation 12:3-4).

John imagined Satan as a dragon, lunging with his tail as he fell from heaven and dislodging a third of the stars from the sky. The stars refer to the angels. In reality the fall of Satan was not a solitary protest. It was a big-time rebellion. And no doubt it is on the basis of his unprecedented "success" in this first battle that the Enemy projects his ultimate victory. A third of the heavenly host is already behind him. The rest, he assures himself, must soon follow.

How did Satan persuade so many of the angelic beings to join him? Earthly revolts give us an insight into the kind of horse trading that was going on in the corridors of heaven. Lucifer would have offered all kinds of incentives. He would have promised the equivalent of promotions and bonuses, stock options, a company jet, free skiing in St. Moritz, and a key to the executive washroom. Every rank—thrones, dominions, principalities, and powers—would have been offered an appropriate reward.

> The Enemy promises the best and pays the worst.
> He promises pleasure and pays with pain. He
> promises life and pays in the currency of death.

Nothing has changed in that respect. Countless millions of people throughout the world today still fall for those same lies. The same Enemy promises the best and pays the worst. He promises honor and pays with dishonor. He promises pleasure and pays with pain. He promises profit and pays with loss. He promises life and pays in the currency of death. It's the same Enemy. And a third of all the heavenly host went with him.

But just in case this begins to look like a formidable achievement, let us keep things in proportion. Even if one-third of the heavenly host joined the opposition, it still means that for every demon harassing you, there are two angels to give you protection. Glory to God!

Three Things We Need to Know About the Enemy's Infernal Hierarchy

1. The Enemy's forces retain all their God-given powers.

When Lucifer was thrown out of heaven, he set up his kingdom and government on the only model he knew. He had been right there in the presence of God. Day and night he had been before the throne. He had observed how God worked. So that's what he copied. He patterned his own administration after God's. In Ephesians 6:12 (NKJV), the famous passage about spiritual warfare, Paul wrote the following:

> For we do not wrestle against flesh and blood, but against principalities, against powers, against the rulers of the darkness of this age, against spiritual hosts of wickedness in the heavenly places.

Notice that the fourfold hierarchy of angels described in Colossians 1:16 is mirrored almost exactly in this fourfold hierarchy of demonic forces: *principalities, powers, rulers of the darkness,* and *spiritual hosts of wickedness.* This is no accident. The titles vary a little, but the structure is the same. Four levels of demonic leadership, with Satan at the top (or, if you prefer, at the *bottom*).

Satan may have lost his innocence when he fell, but he did not lose his intelligence. Like their heavenly counterparts, these fallen angels all have their own personalities. They have their own distinct characteristics. They are immortal and are not limited by time or space. The difference is that they worship Lucifer instead of the living God.

2. The Enemy has agents on your case.

Keep in mind that although Satan stands at the head of a hierarchy, and although he thinks himself divine, he is not God. His minions may have the same capabilities as the heavenly angels, but Satan cannot fully emulate his Creator.

For example, he is not omnipresent. Unlike God, who is present throughout his creation, Satan cannot be everywhere at the same time. He cannot be at your house and at my house at one and the same moment. So what does he do? Simple. He uses his demons. With the exception of Christ's temptation, where he turned up in person, Satan does not perform day-to-day temptation and harassment any more than the CEO of Microsoft or General Electric would answer calls at the company switchboard. He leaves such routine matters to his underlings.

But do not relax your guard on that account. These creatures will do anything they can, try any ploy at their disposal, to harass you, to frustrate you, to oppress you. Paul said that our fight is not against flesh and blood. That's true. But neither is it against a vague principle of evil, as the liberals would have us believe. Demons are conscious, active, and deeply committed to their task.

We are not dealing with people who punch the clock at 8:00 in the morning, enjoy a half-hour lunch and two coffee breaks, and then punch out at 4:30 in the afternoon. We are not dealing with people who take six months' vacation twice a year. We are not dealing with people on welfare, able to sit back and wait for their next government check. I wish that were the case.

Demons are well disciplined, well armed, and blindly obedient soldiers of Satan. You have to be vigilant. You cannot afford to say to yourself, *Now I can let my guard down for a moment, because Satan and his demons are somewhere else.*

Demons have a lot of advantages. Possessing spiritual bodies, they are not limited to space and time. They can dog your footsteps, lay traps for you, shadow you everywhere you go. They will try to undermine your plans. They will invade your prayer life. They will interrupt your thoughts. They will hinder your testimony and discourage you in every way they know how. And very often they will use your friends and family to do it.

3. The Enemy is within.

A man went to a costume party some years ago dressed up as the devil. He had on a full-length red leotard, complete with horns and a tail. On his way to the party, his car broke down on a country road. The only light he could see came from a building across the field, a church, so he set off to knock on the door, forgetting how he was dressed and thinking, *These Christian folks can help me fix my car*. As soon as he stepped through the door though, everyone panicked. They rushed through the windows and out the back door, until only one person was left—a little old lady, standing there defiantly with her cane. He looked at her. She looked at him. Then she pointed her cane at him and said, "Now listen, devil. I may have been a member of this church for fifty years, but I've been on your side all that time!"

This may be a funny story, but many Christians of all ages and backgrounds allow themselves to be used by the Enemy.

It is the saddest thing. Christians who do not resist the devil, who do not flee from temptation, are in effect fraternizing with the Enemy. Have you thought about that? In any regular army, assisting the enemy is an act of treason. You get court-martialed and shot. Yet how many professing Christians are guilty of spiritual treason? How many professing Christians act in a way that wounds or troubles believers? Perhaps it's not deliberate; they would probably be shocked to know that a demon helped put the thought into their minds. But that's the way it is in the invisible war. We are not only soldiers, we are also the battleground.

> Christians who do not resist the devil,
> who do not flee from temptation, are in
> effect fraternizing with the Enemy.

After I preached this message at The Church of The Apostles, a close friend and founding member of the church came to me afterward and said, "Do you think Satan was using me ten years ago when I told you not to start this church?" It was not my place to answer the question directly. But I quoted to him the passage from the Gospels where Peter, in all good faith, tried to prevent Jesus' death on the cross:

> And Peter took him aside and began to rebuke him, saying, "Far be it from you, Lord! This shall never happen to you." But he turned and said to Peter, "Get behind me, Satan! You are a hindrance to me. For you are not setting your mind on the things of God, but on the things of man" (Matthew 16:22-23).

Peter had not planned to go against his Master. And although he was focused on "the things of man" in this attempt to prevent Jesus from dying, he certainly had not figured the Enemy into the equation. Nevertheless, Satan was using him. And if he can use Peter, surely he can use any of us.

LIVING IN THE WAR ZONE

By now you may be thinking, *This is frightening.* And it is—to someone who does not belong to Jesus. But it should not be frightening to the child of God. This is the most important news. Because faithful servants of God—who are not quenching or grieving the Holy Spirit, who are not living in constant disobedience to God and to the Word of God—have God's angels watching over them and empowering them to go from victory to victory.

You may not be able to see them, but God's angelic beings are surrounding you. They are executing the will of God on your behalf. They are faithfully standing beside you to preserve you, to keep you, to sustain you until you get to heaven. They do this because you are an heir of salvation, you are a prince or princess, a child of the King.

> You may not be able to see them, but God's angelic beings are surrounding you. They are executing the will of God on your behalf.

Does the Enemy's organization hold any lessons for us? I think so. Our knowledge of the Enemy's command structure should immediately encourage us in two areas.

1. Prayer

In my office I have a painting, given to me many years ago by my daughter Sarah. It shows a father kneeling beside his son's bed, praying. Outside the window demons are trying to get in, but an angel of the Lord is blocking their way.

As a parent I want to convince you of the importance of prayer. Get on your knees. Pray for your children. Intercede for them and offer the sacrifice of praise and thanksgiving for them, even as Job did, because when you do, the angels of God will foil the demons' plans. As long as you are faithful in prayer, the Enemy will flee.

Have you ever read that in a book on parenting? Not in any book I've seen. I have nothing against books. I love books. I write books. And I would advise parents to read as many as they can get their hands on. But there is a whole set of spiritual issues that most parenting books simply do not address.

So when I hear someone say, "Oh, Dr. So-and-so has come up with a new book that tells you everything you need to know," I get suspicious. Read all the books you can, but recognize that if you do not spend time on your knees, praying, interceding, and even crying before God, you cannot give your children the help and protection they really need.

2. Obedience

We do not have balance in the Christian community. On one side we have people in the mainline church, and beyond the mainline church, who prefer to think Satan and his hordes do not exist. On the other side we have people who say, "All you need to do is cast out demons, and everything is fine." Clearly the second view is closer to the truth. But stating it that way gives the impression that once the demons are cast out, everything will be hunky-dory and the devil will not so much as sneeze in your direction until you reach glory.

Take my word for it: Satan is not so easily scared off. Before you know it, he will be up and at you again, and he will get the better of you if you have not made a thoroughgoing commitment of obedience to Jesus Christ and closed all those doors I talked about earlier.

I decided to write this book to put forward a balanced and biblical view of the Enemy, a view that affirms the existence of the devil but also affirms that obedience will close him out. *Expect* that Satan will attack you, but don't lock the front door to your soul while leaving all the windows open. Because if you have a weak point, Satan will find it.

For example, no matter who you are or how long you spend in prayer, sooner or later a demon called *past sins* is going to come knocking. He will do this by stirring up memories of all the things you have done wrong in the past, either reminding you of how enjoyable they were or making you feel guilty about them. Here is how you deal with him. Remind *him* of something. Remind him of his future, because the Bible says that the lake of fire was specially prepared for the devil and his angels. *Your* past sins don't matter. *His do.*

Similarly, if a demon comes along whose name is *fear*, take up the sword of the Spirit and tell him about the promises of God for you, such as

> "The LORD is on my side; I will not fear.
>   What can man do to me?"
>   (Psalm 118:6)

Remind the Enemy of Jesus' promise to you as one of his followers, "Fear not, little flock, for it is your Father's good pleasure to give you the kingdom" (Luke 12:32).

When a demon called *worry* comes to you and loads you with the cares of this world, tell the Enemy, "My Jesus said not to worry about tomorrow, because tomorrow will worry about itself" (see Matthew 6:34). That's how you have the victory.

The thing you *should not* do is forget about Satan, any more than a soldier at the front can afford to forget about his counterpart on the other side of the line. If you blithely go your way, working hard, not spending time filling your heart and mind with the Word, playing hard and hardly praying, you will find that in a very short time—weeks, even days—demons have come through the doors you have left open. Before you know it, your Christian walk will be collapsing like a soufflé.

Obey. Do not take the mercy and grace of God for granted. Do not give room to the Enemy to work in you and through you. But if you do, remember that all is not lost. For that is another illusion the Enemy would like to sell you. No Christian is perfect. We all progress in the kingdom by a winding path. What matters is to line up behind your Commander in Chief. If you step out of line and get hit, do not stay there. Do not have a pity party. Just get back in line and say, "Forgive me. I'm going to walk behind you again"—and God will give you the victory.

Do not take the mercy and grace of God
for granted. Do not give room to the Enemy
to work in you and through you.

Every time he catches you out, the Enemy unintentionally does you a favor: He alerts you to a weakness in your defenses. So when you stumble, take it to God. Ask, "Lord, what's going on?" He will show you something in your life that is not lining up with his will, something that allows the Enemy a place to enter. Then close the doors.

No one in the Enemy's chain of command can break down a closed door.

PART TWO

KNOW HOW
THE ENEMY FIGHTS

CHAPTER 4

THE ENEMY WANTS YOU

At the end of his first epistle, Peter, the earliest leader of the church, wrote these words:

> Be sober-minded; be watchful. Your adversary the devil prowls around like a roaring lion, seeking someone to devour. Resist him, firm in your faith, knowing that the same kinds of suffering are being experienced by your brotherhood throughout the world (1 Peter 5:8-9).

Those who know the world of wild animals say there are three occasions when a lion roars. First, he roars when a competitor strays into his territory and tries to hunt there. The roar says to intruders, "This is my territory. Get out of here. And stay out."

Second, he roars if he's caught in a storm. Apparently lions dislike the crash of thunder and the flash of lightning.

Third—and this is what I believe Peter was referring to in his epistle—the lion roars after he has caught his prey. He has brought an animal to the ground, and he roars his triumph. He is saying, "I've got you!"

You could conclude from Peter's words that we Christians are perched in a tall tree with the devil roaring at us from below, just as dogs bark at a cat they cannot reach. But this is not the way lions behave. Lions do not roar as they are stalking or chasing their prey. They never announce their arrival by trying to frighten the prey. Their method is to get as close as they can without being seen—so close that even if the quarry sees them, it's too late—and then to pounce.

The devil "prowls around," the Bible tells us. Quietly. Cunningly. Waiting for his moment. Saving his roar until he has his victim pinned down and there is no escape.

The image of Satan that Peter gave us is not a comfortable one. It isn't meant to be comfortable. It's meant to keep us alert.

SATAN THE ADVERSARY

If your faith in God through Jesus Christ is genuine, Satan is your enemy whether you like it or not. You cannot just keep your head down and pretend the conflict is not happening. You are in the middle of it! Satan is *your* adversary. You and I developed this adversarial relationship with Satan the day we said yes to Jesus. At that very instant of surrender, you antagonized Satan. You insulted him. By being snatched from the jaws of death and hell, you have kicked Satan in the teeth—and he will never forgive you for it.

There is no neutrality in Satan's attitude toward you. He thought he had you in the bag—but now you're free. When someone escapes from his realm, Satan does not just shrug his shoulders and say, "Never mind, he won't be missed." He will go after you with a vengeance. Literally. Not in person, of course, for remember that Satan is not omnipresent and cannot be everywhere at once. But he *does* have countless demonic assistants, and he is well organized. So he will enlist demons to work on your case and will devise strategies thinking that he can win you back.

You probably sense this already. If your experiences are anything like mine, you'll agree with me that the Enemy greets you every single morning and keeps working on you every hour of the day. He uses his fallen angels to dog you and create havoc in your life. He wants to stop you from living a life of faith, to stop you from living a life of obedience to God and his Word. He wants to separate you from the provision of God, the mercy of God, and the grace of God. Always remember that you are in enemy territory. I said in the last chapter that the Bible calls Satan "the god of this world" (2 Corinthians 4:4). That's exactly right; in this part of the created order, Satan rules. Christian believers are an invading force. We have established a beachhead, established a foothold, but danger is all around us. Never forget that we are surrounded by unseen adversaries, and they are seeking to harass us.

> Always remember that you are in enemy territory.
> We have established a beachhead, established
> a foothold, but danger is all around us.

You get in the car with your spouse, and the devil is there. When your spouse is sitting beside you, the Enemy is in the middle—even if you can't see him. You go to church, and he's right there with you. Some people think they leave the demons outside when they go to church. Forget it. Satan and his hordes go in there with you so they can start talking to your mind. As the Word of God gets planted in your heart, Satan tries to snatch it away.

It may be happening to you right now as you read this book. These demons are saying to you, "Don't believe this stuff about Satan. He doesn't really exist. You've got enough problems without having to worry about a personal devil. Just forget about it. You're a decent person. You don't have to worry about Satan."

Beware of negotiating with Satan. You run the same risk a hunter did one day when he saw a huge grizzly bear. He lifted his gun to his shoulder and was about to pull the trigger, when the bear spoke. To his surprise, it had a soft, almost hypnotic voice. The bear said, "Hey, isn't it better to talk than to shoot? Why don't we sit down? Let's negotiate this matter. What do you really want?"

The hunter lowered his gun. He thought about it, then said, "Well, all I really want is a fur coat."

"A fur coat?" the bear said. "No problem. That's good. I think it's something we can talk about. For my part, all I want is a full stomach. Really, I'm hopeful we can reach a mutually satisfying compromise."

And so they talked it over. They started negotiating.

You don't parley with Satan any more than you sit down to discuss terms with a grizzly. The idea that everyone has a bit of the truth and all we need to do is fit it together like a jigsaw puzzle has brought the mainline churches to their knees. Because Satan is not really interested in compromise. It's just his way of ensnaring us. Which is why, after a little while, the talk between the hunter and the grizzly came to an end, and the grizzly was seen leaving on his own. Through negotiation he had managed both to fill his stomach and give the hunter a fur coat.

Satan means business. When you and I go to sleep at night, he's still burning the midnight oil, making plans for the next day. In the middle of the night the lion is still prowling, pacing up and down, hungry, determined to get his prey. After all, lions don't stalk their quarry for the fun of it. They don't sneak up on us so we can take photographs of them. The devil is waiting for you to grow spiritually lazy—and when you do, he will move with lightning speed. Right after he brings his prey under him, he will roar, as if to say, "I've got you!" He will roar the roar of victory, which will tell everybody else, "Stay out of here! She's mine! He's mine! Now leave me alone so I can enjoy the fruits of my kill."

That roar is a challenge to Almighty God. Satan says, "God, look at the devastation I've brought on one of your children." For remember, Satan's aim, from his first rebellion, has been to take God's place.

> "You said in your heart,
>   'I will ascend to heaven;
>   above the stars of God

> I will set my throne on high;
> I will sit on the mount of assembly
> in the far reaches of the north;
> I will ascend above the heights of the clouds;
> I will make myself like the Most High.'"
> (Isaiah 14:13-14)

He has never given up that ambition. And every battle, every skirmish he wins in the invisible war, every success he scores in undermining your faith and witness, makes him more certain that one day he will achieve his ultimate goal. In his delusion, Satan thinks he has taken another step closer to removing God from the throne so he can rule the universe himself.

This is why Peter gave us this essential advice: "Be sober, be vigilant; because your adversary the devil walks about like a roaring lion."

Why did Peter say to be sober? We're all aware of the misery caused by drunk driving. I have buried young people who were its victims, and it is heartbreaking beyond words. Drunk driving is a major cause of death on our roads. A drunk person is incapable of accurately assessing his ability to drive safely. He has impaired vision. He has impaired reactions. He has impaired control of his limbs. And yet he *feels* like a superman. Drunkenness creates the ultimate form of self-deception.

Sin, said Peter, is *like drunkenness*. It can numb our spiritual senses to the point of making us deny the existence of a spiritual war. People who are not spiritually sober are unable to see things clearly from God's perspective. They do not live by a set of biblical values.

Do not be flippant about the Enemy. The Enemy wants to destroy you. That's his intention.

Peter told believers to be serious-minded about the devil. To be serious-minded about the invisible war. To be serious-minded about the traps the Enemy sets up to ensnare the unwary. Do not be flippant about the Enemy if you are a child of God and walking with Jesus Christ. Do not be flippant, because the Enemy wants to destroy you, to destroy your family, to destroy your business, to destroy everything you touch. That's his intention. He wants *you*.

But of course you are not the *only* one the Enemy wants. Christians and Christian leaders down through the ages have been the focus of his attention, and plenty of prominent believers in Scripture have fallen to Satan's temptations.

PROMINENT BELIEVERS HAVE ALSO FALLEN

Let's look at some of the believers in the Bible who gave in to Satan.

Joshua Lost Because He Was Overconfident

Everyone knows the story of Joshua and the battle of Jericho. How the people of Israel came up to take this strongly fortified city. How God gave Joshua the instruction not to attack head-on, but to march around Jericho seven times—a strange military tactic, to say the least. And how at the end of seven circuits the Israelites blew their trumpets and the city's fortifications collapsed.

Yet not so many have read what happened next. The Bible tells us:

> So the LORD was with Joshua, and his fame was in all the land.
>
> But the people of Israel broke faith in regard to the devoted things, for Achan the son of Carmi, son of Zabdi, son of Zerah, of the tribe of Judah, took some of the devoted things. And the anger of the LORD burned against the people of Israel (Joshua 6:27–7:1).

Flushed with victory, unaware of the sin in Israel, and feeling overconfident, Joshua sent spies up to the next city. Just how blasé the Israelites had become can be judged from the spies' advice, and Joshua's credulity in following it. The spies said,

> "Do not have all the people go up, but let about two or three thousand men go up and attack Ai. Do not make the whole people toil up there, for they are few" (Joshua 7:3).

Joshua underestimated both the resilience of the men of Ai and the devastating impact of Israel's sin. The raiding party was repulsed with thirty-six fatalities, and Joshua was reduced to despair. He fell before God and cried out,

> "O Lord, what can I say, when Israel has turned their backs before their enemies! For the Canaanites and all the inhabitants of the land will hear of it and will surround us and cut off our name from the earth. And what will you do for your great name?" (7:8-9).

God, though, brought this self-pity quickly to heel. "The LORD said to Joshua, 'Get up! Why have you fallen on your face?'" (7:10).

The source of the problem was soon uncovered. During the plundering of Jericho, one of the Israelites had gone against God's specific command and had committed a sin of greed. He finally confessed:

> And Achan answered Joshua, "Truly I have sinned against the LORD God of Israel, and this is what I did: When I saw among the spoil a beautiful cloak from Shinar, and 200 shekels of silver, and a bar of gold weighing 50 shekels, then I coveted them and took them. And see, they are hidden in the earth inside my tent, with the silver underneath" (7:20-21).

The Israelites quickly found these items, which cleansed the people of their sin. Ai fell soon afterward.

You might think that was the end of the episode. But no sooner had Joshua routed Ai than he was fooled into signing a treaty with the Gibeonites. Once again Joshua acted impulsively. The people of Israel did what they thought was best, but "did not ask counsel from the LORD" (Joshua 9:14). The results of this mistake were severe. Joshua should have destroyed the Gibeonites, but by swearing in the name of God that he would spare them, he tied God's hands and compromised Israel's long-term security. You can almost hear the roar of Satan: "I got your man. I got your man."

Success and overconfidence go in the motion of a pendulum. One swings into the other and back again. Beware when you have scored a victory over the Enemy; that is precisely the time when you are most at risk.

> Beware when you have scored a victory
> over the Enemy; that is precisely the
> time when you are most at risk.

Joshua fell into temptation. So did that great man of God, King David.

David Fell Because He Ceased to Be Vigilant

I advise you to spend a few minutes reading 2 Samuel 11, because it will teach you a lot about temptation. If ever a man seemed to deserve trust, loyalty, and confidence, it was David, a man blessed by God, a man distinguished for being "after God's own heart," a king of Israel at the peak of his powers. And yet in this passage we see him behaving in a way that was not only unstatesmanlike but downright villainous. He made a single satanically inspired decision, and from that determination flowed a foul river of lust, covetousness, adultery, intrigue, betrayal, and finally, murder.

His decision is described in just five words: "But David remained at Jerusalem" (2 Samuel 11:1). Doesn't sound like much, does it? David took some time off. He let Joab, his chief of staff, take care of destroying Ammon and besieging Rabbah while he went back to his palace.

The Bible does not give us a reason. Maybe David was tired. Maybe he had other business. Maybe he wanted to test Joab's leadership qualities. We just don't know. But however innocent the motives, this decision was fatal. It took David away from his primary responsibilities of leadership, and he ceased to be sober and vigilant. He did not hear the lion creeping toward him. He was not prepared for the temptation. But one night he couldn't sleep. He got up—and the trap was there, ready to spring.

When you have a sleepless night, what do you do? Do you get up and watch television, or do you get on your knees and begin to bless God and pray? Do you allow your mental DVD player to rehearse the past day's problems, or do you sing praises and bless the name of God?

Almost every day we are presented with options like this. Every moment that is not consciously dedicated to some godly end is available for the devil to use. It is like blank space to doodle in, a silent interlude to be filled with noise. That's why one of the best ways to avoid being tempted is to fill your mind and attention with some positive and constructive project. If David had walked across the street, he would have been in God's temple. He would have been safe. But no:

> It happened, late one afternoon, when David arose from his couch and was walking on the roof of the king's house, that he saw from the roof a woman bathing; and the woman was very beautiful (2 Samuel 11:2).

The whole sorry tale of David's sin unfolded from that moment. He made inquiries about the woman. He discovered her identity. He slept with her. She got pregnant. He attempted to disguise his adultery by bringing her husband, Uriah, back from the war and getting him drunk so he would sleep with her. Finally, when Uriah proved more pious than David and refused to sleep with his own wife lest he endanger the war effort, David cold-bloodedly arranged his death.

By then, however, David had long been in Satan's control. When he walked up the stairs to the roof of the king's house—when his eyes fell on the woman and his heartbeat quickened—Satan sprang his trap and roared, "God, I got your choicest." After that, the rest was inevitable. I will not dwell on the consequences. Suffice it to say that, through a moment's loss of sobriety and vigilance, David brought tragedy to his kingdom and dishonor to the name of his God.

Joshua fell, David fell, and so did Simon Peter.

Peter Fell Because He Underestimated His Character Flaws

If you are ever tempted to think you've blown it—that Satan has finally and irrevocably dragged you away from God—reflect on the life of Simon Peter.

> If you are ever tempted to think you've blown it—
> that Satan has finally and irrevocably dragged you
> away from God—reflect on the life of Simon Peter.

Peter's faith was strong and straightforward. And at the end of Jesus' earthly ministry, after Jesus had gathered his disciples around him for the Last Supper, Peter expressed that faith with typical enthusiasm and thoughtlessness. "Lord," he said, "I am ready to go with you both to prison and to death" (Luke 22:33). They had just shared the precious Passover meal, in which Jesus had revealed that he himself was the Passover Lamb and that he was going to die for the redemption and salvation of humankind.

But this was not what inspired Peter's outburst. Right before he affirmed his faith in Jesus, the Lord had said:

"Simon, Simon, behold, Satan demanded to have you,
that he might sift you like wheat, but I have prayed for
you that your faith may not fail. And when you have
turned again, strengthen your brothers" (Luke 22:31-32).

If you're a city slicker, you may not appreciate what is meant by that phrase "sift you like wheat." That is not an enjoyable process. The sieve is a round implement made of wood, about twenty-four inches in diameter, sometimes bigger, with a fine wire mesh across the bottom. The person doing the sifting puts the wheat into the sieve, along with the chaff and the dirt and everything else, and then begins to shake it vigorously, throwing the contents into the air so that the chaff can be blown away. In Peter's case—so Satan's request implies—very little wheat would be left. And even with Jesus praying for him, the sifting was pretty thorough.

I do not have to tell you what happened. During Jesus' trial, Peter, who had promised to go with Jesus to prison and to death, was so scared that he denied even *knowing* his Lord and Master. And he did it—not once, not twice, but three times—as Jesus had predicted. "And immediately, while he was still speaking, the rooster crowed" (Luke 22:60). Peter had fallen right into Satan's trap, despite Jesus' warning. He had been vigilant for his Lord but not vigilant for his own weakness of character. You can almost hear the lion's roar behind the cock's crow. Satan was shouting, "God, I've got the chief apostle of your Son. I've got him!"

Peter, the Bible tells us, went out and wept bitterly. Yet his sifting had just started. After the sifting of fear came the sifting of self-doubt and self-hatred. I wonder if Peter thought of suicide. He had betrayed his friend in a way that was not much different from that of Judas. He had become utterly useless.

Isn't that exactly what it's like to be depressed? As if life has come to an end. How many Christians have been trapped in those feelings? But note that Peter knew how to repent, unlike Judas, who by now had scattered his thirty pieces of silver and hung himself. Repentance is the answer. "And when you have turned again," Jesus said, "strengthen your brothers." Peter clung to those words, and after the resurrection, he obeyed them.

Let's look at one more example—one of the most disturbing instances of satanic attack in the New Testament.

Ananias and Sapphira Fell Because They Purposely Lied

We read in the book of Acts, chapter 5, that the believers were selling their possessions and putting the money at the feet of the apostles. They were giving everything, for these were trying times. Their enemies were throwing Christians out of their houses, out of their jobs, and out of their communities because of their faith. They had no option but to rely on one another for everything.

Most of them had witnessed Jesus' resurrection. And you would think that if any group of people deserved to be called sober and vigilant, this would be it. Yet two of them, a man by the name of Ananias and his wife, Sapphira, sold a piece of land and then secretly withheld a portion of the proceeds. They had accepted Jesus as their Lord and Savior. They were committed enough to sell their land, but they were afraid. They wanted security. They left open the doors of fear and deception, and the Enemy got in.

Listen to what happened when Ananias tried to lay his gift at the apostles' feet:

> But Peter said, "Ananias, why has Satan filled your heart to lie to the Holy Spirit and to keep back for yourself part of the proceeds of the land? While it remained unsold, did it not remain your own? And after it was sold, was it not at your disposal? Why is it that you have contrived this deed in your heart? You have not lied to man but to God" (Acts 5:3-4).

Unlike David, whose initial sin seems to have been unpremeditated, Ananias and Sapphira sinned deliberately, with careful preparation. Also their sin appears to have had more immediate and more dire consequences: "When Ananias heard these words, he fell down and breathed his last" (5:5). The same fate befell his wife three hours later. This raises an important question: Can Satan really devour God's children, even depriving them of their salvation?

The story of Ananias and Sapphira is ambiguous on this point. But turn to the first epistle of John, where the apostle wrote:

> We know that everyone who has been born of God does
> not keep on sinning, but he who was born of God protects
> him, and the evil one does not touch him (1 John 5:18).

A fuller translation of the word *touch* is "sever the vital union." In other words, John said Satan cannot break the cord of salvation linking the Christian believer to God. Even the careless believer, the believer who repeatedly forgets to be sober and vigilant, cannot lose his salvation.

God has spoken, and Satan is powerless to change it. *But*—and this is a big but—Satan can devour almost everything else. Your peace of mind. Your effectiveness. Your witness. Your health. Your friendships. Your marriage. Your work. Everything. All of this can be devoured by the roaring lion. The devil not only roars, he has teeth. He can chew you up so thoroughly, your entire Christian life is a write-off.

God has spoken, and Satan is powerless to
change it. But Satan can devour almost everything
else. The devil not only roars, he has teeth.

Peter did not write, "The devil is a paper tiger." Paul did not say to the Ephesians, "Lay aside the armor of God, you won't need it." James did not tell Christians, "Don't bother resisting the devil, he'll never even come near you." Instead we are urged over and over again to resist the devil, to be spiritually sober and vigilant, to put on the armor of God, to live every day in God's fullness, and to pray every day in the Spirit. On the basis of those commands, we have authority over the devil.

I have often heard a statement attributed to the great German Reformer Martin Luther that advises us to make fun of Satan: "The best way to drive out the devil, of course, is through using the Scripture, but if he will not yield to the text of the Scripture, then jeer at him, flout him, for he cannot bear scorn." After all, it is Satan who is going to end up in the lake of fire, not us. Ultimately the joke is on him.

Yet the enemy has not given up; he works very hard to keep us weak.

HOW THE ENEMY KEEPS US WEAK

Many Christians in America are stuck in neutral and are unproductive. They are saved, but their Christian walk is going nowhere, like a car with its wheels mired in the mud. This is profoundly satisfying to the Enemy. Countless troops in God's army have never received their basic training. They're standing on the drill square, flabby, undisciplined, lazy, and afraid.

From the Enemy's point of view, Christians like this are his highest achievement. We learned earlier that Satan cannot undo the work of salvation in a believer. God has spoken, and Satan is powerless to countermand the order. So the Enemy aims for the next best thing—not the believer's soul but the believer's *effectiveness*.

If you could peek at Satan's goal-setting program, you would find that one of his prime objectives is to keep Christians from growing in faith. To keep them from understanding and applying the Word of God in daily life. To keep them in the murky, shallow waters of mediocrity, to keep them focusing on their problems, on their pain, on their worries, on their own little kingdoms. These

Christians will never pose a threat to him. They are soldiers who can't shoot, fighters who can't fight.

One of Satan's prime objectives is to keep Christians from growing in faith. To keep them from understanding and applying the Word of God in daily life.

Jesus warned his followers of this in one of the best-known passages in the Gospels. If you think you know this parable so well that you don't need to read it again, I advise you to pick up your Bible and find Matthew 13:1-9,18-23. You might be surprised at my interpretation of the parable of the soils.

THE PARABLE OF THE SOILS

I can hear you correcting me. Most translations and commentaries entitle this passage The Parable of the Sower. But it is not about the sower. Nor is it about the seed. Very emphatically the focus of Jesus' message is on the *soil*.

There is a good reason for this. Both the sower and the seed are beyond the Enemy's power. The sower is God himself. The seed is God's Word. And the writer of Hebrews told us that "the word of God is living and active, sharper than any two-edged sword, piercing to the division of soul and of spirit, of joints and of marrow, and discerning the thoughts and intentions of the heart" (Hebrews 4:12).

It may surprise you to know that Satan agrees with this. In that sense he is a believer—not because he submits his will to the Holy Spirit (that he absolutely refuses to do), but because bitter experience has proved to him what the Word of God can do. He knows it can change our lives. He knows it can convict us of sin. He knows it can judge and condemn us. He knows it can encourage and uplift us. He knows it can accomplish God's purposes in our lives. Satan does not mess with God's Word any more than you or I would mess with a stick of dynamite.

So the Enemy uses a different tactic. He can't change the sower. He can't change the seed. So he monkeys around with the soil where the seed has to take root, constantly seeking to prevent the Word of God from taking root and growing in Christian hearts.

Three kinds of soil serve the Enemy's purposes.

Soil 1: Seed-Proof Soil

Archaeologists excavating one of Egypt's famous pyramids once discovered a grain of wheat. When they ran tests, they discovered to their surprise that this grain of wheat had been inside that pyramid for nearly three thousand years. All this time it sat there on a hard rock, doing nothing. Yet someone has calculated that if that grain had been planted and harvested, planted and harvested over the same period of time, it would have produced enough bread by now to feed the entire planet for two days!

Look carefully at the first part of the parable of the soils, as explained by Jesus:

> "Hear then the parable of the sower: When anyone hears the word of the kingdom and does not understand it, the evil one comes and snatches away what has been sown in his heart. This is what was sown along the path" (Matthew 13:18-19).

The phrase "along the path" is significant. This soil is not in the middle of the field—it is on the edge. In other words, this soil depicts what is liable to happen to people who keep themselves on the fringes of the church.

What is the nature of such soil? Well, I don't know much about American farming, but I can tell you a little about farming in the Middle East, which Jesus had in mind when he told the parable. Over there, fences or hedgerows do not separate one farm from the next. Between Mr. Hussein's farm and Mr. Ali's farm, you will find a narrow pathway, a strip of land, which the repeated pressure of feet and hooves has compacted into such a hard crust that even rainwater fails to penetrate it. In its natural state this kind of soil is not ready to receive seed. If any seeds fall on it, they just sit there, exposed, unnourished, unshaded, waiting like peas on a dinner plate until a hungry bird swoops down and eats them.

Notice how Jesus explains this part of the parable. This kind of soil is like the people who *hear* the Word of God but *do not understand it.* They get some goose bumps around Christmastime. They get teary-eyed when a tragedy strikes somewhere. Otherwise their hearts are as hard as rock. They may go to church on occasion. They may even read the Bible. But nothing is getting through.

Perhaps those "along the path" figure they know everything the Bible says already, so they don't need to listen. Perhaps they have such fixed ideas about God, they refuse to listen to anything new. Perhaps they can't concentrate for more than a few seconds. Or, it may be they forget what they've heard as soon as they hear it.

All these subterfuges are part of the Enemy's strategy to produce hardness of heart. And none of us is immune. With the help of his demons, Satan will try to make sure that God's Word flies in one ear and out the other. He will try to stop us from applying the Word of God to an upcoming business decision. He will try to make us substitute human wisdom for God's Word, psychology for scriptural teaching, or counseling for the power of the Holy Spirit. In all these ways he will attempt to snatch the seed of God's Word from us before it has the chance to grow and bear fruit.

> Satan will try to make us substitute human wisdom
> for God's Word, psychology for scriptural teaching,
> or counseling for the power of the Holy Spirit.

He will do this very quickly. If you have visited the Middle East, you have noticed the ravens. They go around and around, searching for something to take, then suddenly—*whack!*—they snatch it and fly off. Those who have the spiritual seed snatched from them in this way may develop a sense of restlessness and dissatisfaction.

I have known people who go from church to church, from teacher to teacher, from counselor to counselor, from seminar to seminar, from retreat to retreat—yet nothing is happening inside. Satan has convinced them, "All you need is more seed, more seed, more seed," when in reality the problem is not the seed but the soil. They need the plowing of the Holy Spirit to break up the soil of their hearts and allow the Word of God to take root.

How does this first type of soil turn seed-proof?

1. Through sin

The psalmist said,

> "If I had cherished iniquity in my heart,
>   the Lord would not have listened."
> (Psalm 66:18)

If there is a sin in our lives, and we've rationalized it, all the teaching and preaching in the world will not do us any good. The only way forward is confession and renewal. That's why we start our worship with confession, so we can break the hard soil of our hearts. If there is any hardening there, confession begins to break it down so that God's Word will be able to penetrate.

> If there is a sin in our lives, the only way forward is confession and renewal.

2. Through bitterness

The writer of Hebrews warned Christians against the "root of bitterness" (12:15). It's an apt description, for bitterness goes down deep into the soil of our hearts.

Some plants in the desert areas of the Middle East have adapted to their dry environment by sending roots down through the rocks—forty or fifty feet deep!—to tap subterranean moisture. Such roots are not easily dislodged.

Similarly, to harbor bitterness toward another person creates a fundamental change in the depth of your personality. You become so wrapped up in the injustice you claim has been done to you, you can see little else. Even the Holy Spirit will have trouble getting through. The Word of God will glance off you even if you read it twenty-four hours a day.

3. Through compromised leadership

The average church in America has around 250 members. If the devil wants to reach out to a whole church, he is going to need a minimum of 250 demons to do it—one demon to snatch the Word from each believer's heart. But the devil is a great economist. It's so much more economical to go after the preacher. He will make him preach a lie, while at the same time convincing people that they are hearing an honest exposition of God's Word. That way Satan uses just one demon to achieve exactly the same result. He gets 250 people for the price of one.

That is one reason ministers of the gospel find themselves under attack. A friend told me recently of a struggle at his church. The pastor had been in the same pulpit for twenty-five years. He wasn't preaching a lie, but familiarity with the congregation had left him complacent, and he was no longer challenging or inspiring the membership with the Word of God. Still many members gave him their unqualified support, and when those who could see what was happening felt it was God's will for him to move on, the argument between the two sides almost split the church. Satan was right there, dividing and conquering.

Where Satan's first plan fails, he has a second plan in place: the principle of shallow soil.

Soil 2: Shallow Soil

If Satan cannot prevent the seed from germinating, he will do his best to prevent the soil from nourishing it, leaving the seed vulnerable to extremes of weather.

> "As for what was sown on rocky ground, this is the one who hears the word and immediately receives it with joy, yet he has no root in himself, but endures for a while, and when tribulation or persecution arises on account of the word, immediately he falls away" (Matthew 13:20-21).

This is the person who gets excited about the gospel. He comes down the aisle, signs the decision card, and goes to church for several months afterward. Every time the doors are open, he's there. And then his weakness is exposed.

Receiving the Word carries a cost. Family members begin to make fun of you. They'll say, "Hello, Mr. Preacher" or "Here comes the prophet." Or a colleague at work will find out you have committed your life to the Lord, and he will start telling everyone, "Hey, watch out, here comes the Bible-thumper. Be careful." These remarks are particularly damaging to young people, who are so vulnerable to peer pressure. Their friends tell them, "Well, you're not cool anymore. You're no fun to be with."

Nobody enjoys persecution. So why endure it if it can be avoided? That is what a demon will whisper in your ear. "You know, the smart move is to go underground with your newfound faith. Don't flaunt it. Keep it quiet. That way you won't upset anyone."

I've even heard ministers say: "You need to keep your religion between you and God. After all, religion is meant to be private." Tempting, isn't it? Especially if a church leader gives his stamp of approval. But keeping your faith secret erases your effectiveness for God.

I've seen it happen. Some years ago a couple said to me, "We're leaving your church."

I asked why.

"Our children are not saved," they said, "and when they come home during the holidays and bring their friends, we just find it very embarrassing to take them to The Church of The Apostles. The preaching is so blunt and so hard. We want to take them to a church where they'll hear some abstract sermons."

I said to them at the time, "As a father of four children, I can tell you right out that I would rather see my kids offended and in heaven than appeased and in hell because of abstract sermons. An unsaved person needs to be told he's as lost as a goat in a hailstorm, and that he needs Jesus Christ. If he finds that offensive, God bless him. At least you gave them the opportunity to be exposed to the truth."

Seed-proof soil, shallow soil—if those don't work, Satan uses a third method to keep believers weak: spoiled soil.

Soil 3: Spoiled Soil

As the sower scattered his seed, the parable tells us, "Other seeds fell among thorns, and the thorns grew up and choked them" (Matthew 13:7).

The soil here is perfectly good. It isn't hardened or shallow. It is soft, deep, well-watered. By rights, the seed should thrive in it. And this is exactly why the Enemy works so hard to prevent the seed from growing. His strategy? Make sure there are plenty of *other* seeds in the soil, ready to compete with the seed of the Word. As Jesus explained:

> "As for what was sown among thorns, this is the one who hears the word, but the cares of the world and the deceitfulness of riches choke the word, and it proves unfruitful" (Matthew 13:22).

We usually think of the thorns as worries and material ambition, ensnaring people who cannot let go of their anxieties or who seek security in their net worth rather than in their commitment to Jesus Christ. Most often, though, the thorns are simply *activities*.

Look around the average church, and you will find Christians who are busy, busy, busy—with nothing to show for it. You see, if Satan cannot snatch the seed of the Word away from your heart, if he cannot stunt its growth with persecution, then he will get you so wrapped up in activities, you won't have time to think about growing or reproducing yourself in the kingdom of God. Satan will open up a new job possibility. He will expand your social life. He will get you to play the stock market. He will give you prominence and fame, or co-opt you onto another committee. None of these things are bad—not even the committee. But they are all distractions from our first goal: to grow and bear fruit.

> Look around the average church, and you
> will find Christians who are busy, busy,
> busy—with nothing to show for it.

I speak from experience. In the first two years of The Church of The Apostles, I was run ragged. Finally, in the fall of 1989, the Lord put me flat on my back for two weeks. I couldn't carry on with my activities. Confined to my bed, I had no choice. And the Lord's precious voice was so clear to me. He said, "You cannot minister to others until you have ministered to me."

That blew me away. I thought I was doing my best. I thought it was my *job* to minister to others. I don't mean I missed my devotions. Even at the busiest times I read the Scriptures every day. I prayed. But you see, I had a problem saying no. I took on everything that came my way. And the Lord had to tell me that no matter how hard I worked, I wasn't the fourth member of the Trinity. He also had to remind me that the Holy Spirit did the *real* work. I'd better get my priorities straight because one hour spent in harness with the Holy Spirit achieved more than a year slogging it out on my own.

Ministers are the biggest culprits when it comes to going it alone. The average evangelical American pastor spends less than twenty minutes a day in prayer. His counterpart in South Korea spends at least ninety minutes. Is it any wonder that God is doing great things in South Korea?

The Lord took me away from my activities and made it clear to me that he wanted me to give the first two hours of the day to him—and him alone. If I had not obeyed, if I had not adjusted my lifestyle radically, I honestly believe I would not be around to write this book today.

Activism is Satan's trick, pure and simple. He delights in getting us preoccupied. It doesn't matter what the object of that preoccupation is. Good things will serve just as well as evil. All the Enemy wants is for our attention to be distracted and our strength sapped. And in most of America his strategy is working.

Having lived in three different cultures around the world, I am convinced that Americans think that activity and productiveness are the same thing. It's not that activity is wrong, any more than riches are wrong. Activity is fine as long as it does not become the focus of your life. Riches are fine as long as they do not become your security and your primary goal.

God has given us many good things to enjoy. It is our responsibility as Christians to make sure that we use them correctly, and do not treat them with a single-minded devotion, which turns them from gifts into idols.

> God has given us many good things to enjoy. It is our responsibility to make sure that we use them correctly and do not turn them from gifts into idols.

When the Muslim general Mohammed Ghusani invaded India, his forces went into the Hindu temples and smashed every idol they could find. Islam does not tolerate idols—and Hinduism has many of them. Entering one celebrated temple, Ghusani was confronted by the priests. They pleaded with him, "We beg of you, do not destroy the idol here. This is the holiest of all idols. Please leave it alone." Ghusani took no notice. Pushing the priests aside, he unsheathed his sword and dealt the idol a resounding blow. Immediately it shattered—and a stream of precious stones cascaded from its hollow center.

Our idols are not made of wood or plaster, but they are just as real, and we cling to them just as tenaciously as those Hindu priests. Yet every time we destroy an idol, we gain far more than we lose. For every idol we demolish will bring us new treasures of grace and remove another hindrance to the productive life of prayer.

An effective Christian walk, in which idols are readily disposed of, comes from a soil in which the seed falls, roots, germinates, and bears fruit.

> "As for what was sown on good soil, this is the one who hears the word and understands it. He indeed bears fruit and yields, in one case a hundredfold, in another sixty, and in another thirty" (Matthew 13:23).

This good soil belongs to those who are sober and vigilant, those who are serious-minded about the Enemy and the Enemy's works. They are productive according to the talents and blessings God has given them. They are not all productive to the same degree or in the same way, but their productiveness is in line with God's wider plan for his kingdom. The Enemy wants to neutralize this productiveness so that the forces arrayed against him will be weaker. It is part of our calling as Christians, therefore, to strive to be good soil.

So it's necessary to do some soil testing in your life. If you come to the Word of God with an unrepentant heart, Satan is going to snatch the seed away. If you come to the Word of God harboring bitterness or a fear of being unpopular, your faith will wither. If you come to the Word of God preoccupied with anxieties and activities, your productiveness will be choked. But as you develop a strong and nourishing soil, the good seed of the gospel sown by the Lord Jesus Christ will produce genuine and abundant fruit. When that happens, the Enemy's plan is foiled.

As Christians we *have* to walk in daily submission to Jesus Christ. In that and that alone resides our authority over the devil. We can't be cocky. We can't single-handedly take on the spiritual principalities and powers. The devil, the roaring lion on the prowl, can be defeated only by the power of the Lord Jesus Christ and the blood of the Lamb. For only when you and I line up behind that other, greater lion, the Lion of Judah, and are covered by the shadow of the Almighty and fortified by the whole armor of God, can we expect to be victorious.

CHAPTER 5

CLOSE COMBAT WITH THE ENEMY

During the Second World War, immediately after the collapse of France, Hitler pushed westward to the coast of the English Channel and prepared his assault on the British mainland. He knew that if he was to send ground troops across to invade Britain, he would first have to win the war in the air. And so the Battle of Britain began. Nazi Germany sent massive formations of bombers over British territory, attempting both to destroy ground installations and to knock out the British air defenses. If Germany won air supremacy, the invasion would be easy.

Against these massive forces, the British fighter command used a number of strategies. One of the most important was this: keep above the enemy. Gain higher altitude. Fight from above. So when the radar warned of an imminent attack, and the order came for crews to scramble, Royal Air Force pilots took their planes up as high as they could, as fast as they could. It was one of the reasons Britain won the air battle, and why the invasion, when it came, was an Allied invasion going the other way—from Britain into occupied France.

Fight from above might summarize God's instructions to his people in the invisible war. Because *above* is where Christ is. Turn to Ephesians and see how Paul prayed, that the God of our Lord Jesus Christ, the Father of glory, may give you the Spirit of wisdom and of revelation in the knowledge of him, having the eyes of your hearts enlightened, that you may know what is the hope to which he has called you, what are the riches of his glorious inheritance in the saints, and what is the immeasurable greatness of his power toward us who believe, according to the working of his great might that he worked in Christ when he raised him from the dead and seated him at his right hand in the heavenly places, far above all rule and authority and power and dominion, and above every name that is named, not only in this age but also in the one to come (1:17-21).

When God raised Jesus from the dead, he gave him, in spiritual terms, the highest altitude possible. He sat him above "all rule and authority and power and dominion"—above the entire angelic order, good and evil. He sat him above Satan and his demonic forces. He sat him high above circumstances and chance. He said to Jesus, as the psalmist prophesied,

"Sit at my right hand,
    until I make your enemies your footstool."
                    (Psalm 110:1)

Now you may think this puts Jesus rather far off. After all, there is no higher place than to sit at God's right hand. If ever Scripture gave us an image of the transcendent God, this is it. But look at what Paul went on to say in the next chapter of Ephesians:

But God, being rich in mercy, because of the great love with which he loved us, even when we were dead in our trespasses, made us alive together with Christ—by grace you have been saved—and raised us up with him and seated us with him in the heavenly places in Christ Jesus (2:4-6).

Take a look around you. Where are you? Sitting in an armchair? Out on your veranda? In an airport or a bus station someplace? Forget it—in the reality of the Spirit you are in none of these places. You are up there with Christ Jesus. Those who belong to God, who are born of the Spirit of God and have surrendered their lives to Jesus Christ, are already positioned in heaven. Physically you may be on earth, but spiritually you are with God.

> Those who have surrendered their lives to Jesus
> Christ are already positioned in heaven. Physically
> you may be on earth, but spiritually you are with God.

Isn't that wonderful? That is the blessing God has given us. Unlike the RAF pilots of the Second World War, we have altitude already. We don't have to jump into airplanes to achieve it. We're already there. As heirs of the everlasting kingdom we already occupy ground that is inaccessible to the Enemy. We are already in that one place from which we can successfully attack and resist the devil. From this vantage point we make Satan and all his minions vulnerable. We have the victory because we are where Christ is.

THE ENEMY'S TACTICS

How does the Enemy hope to attack and overcome you when you are, in effect, beyond the range of his biggest guns? Let me give you another example from the pages of military history.

Not many people have successfully invaded the British Isles. Hitler failed. Napoleon failed. To find the last time anyone brought an army across to British shores you have to go back to the year every school student in Britain knows by heart—the year 1066. At that time what we today call England was populated by the Anglo-Saxons and ruled by King Harold. You probably know the story already. The Normans crossed the channel under the leadership of

William the Conqueror, trounced the Anglo-Saxons at the Battle of
Hastings, during which Harold took an arrow in the eye, and then
proceeded to overrun the country.

What many people don't know is that the Battle of Hastings was
a very close contest. Harold was no pushover. He had carefully positioned his troops at the top of a long ridge, giving them such a strong
positional advantage that after several hours of fighting, the Normans had been all but beaten off. What turned the battle around?
William changed tactics. He told his captains to fake a retreat. The
effect was to make Harold lose control of his army. Thinking they
had won, they abandoned the ridge and ran down the slope in pur-
suit of the retreating Normans. They fell into a trap. For as soon
as they were down on level ground, the Normans turned on them.
Stronger and better equipped, the Normans now had the advantage.
And they pressed it home.

This is the Enemy's principal tactic: to draw you down from the
strategic high ground so he can fight you on the level. While you
remain in the heavenly places you have an overwhelming advantage. As soon as you come down to the Enemy's level, the advantage belongs to him.

And believe me, he will use it ruthlessly. He will employ any
means he can think of to pull you down from the ridge of faithful
obedience to God, for as soon as you leave the ridge he can make
you forget that he is vulnerable, make you forget that he is a defeated
foe. He can neutralize you.

> This is the Enemy's principal tactic: to draw
> you down from the strategic high ground
> so he can fight you on the level.

Please concentrate here, because this may be the most crucial
point. When it comes to direct combat, the Enemy has three ways

of bringing you down. To return to an image I used earlier, he concentrates on three particular doors into your soul. The apostle John outlined them for us in his first epistle:

> Do not love the world or the things in the world. If anyone loves the world, the love of the Father is not in him. For all that is in the world—the lust of the flesh, the lust of the eyes, and the pride of life—is not of the Father but is of the world. And the world is passing away, and the lust of it; but he who does the will of God abides forever (1 John 2:15-17 NKJV).

The lust of the flesh, the lust of the eyes, the pride of life. These things are of the world, and because they are of the world, they are of the Enemy, who rules this world. Every kind of sin falls into one of these three categories. The lust of the flesh is the craving to satisfy our appetites. The lust of the eyes is the craving for what belongs to others—the sin of covetousness. The pride of life is the decision to step outside of biblical teaching, either to justify our sinful behavior, or—more subtly—to pursue what we think is the will of God.

Together these three doors often form a demonic progression. First, we pay attention to the urgings of our fallen nature. Second, we seek to gratify those urges by taking what we should not have. And third, we seek to render these urges legitimate by rationalizing them and casting off restraint. As we move along the progression, the devil captures, in turn, our passions, our ego, and our will.

You can see exactly this sequence in the story of David's affair with Uriah's wife, Bathsheba. David fell first by submitting to his passions—allowing the sight of Bathsheba to ignite his lust. He fell a second time by coveting her, even though she was another man's wife. He fell a third time, and most seriously, when he tried to disguise her pregnancy by calling Uriah back from the war to sleep with her. By then he was in up to his neck. He wanted Bathsheba so badly he was ready to order her husband's death. One sin paved the way for the next.

You can almost see the demons plotting behind the scenes, moving David along, stage by stage, until he was in so deep he couldn't get out. For it is the conquest of your *will* that the Enemy most desires. If he has your will, he has everything he can get—short of your salvation. But more of that in a moment.

First, I want to examine each kind of door by looking at the example of the person who suffered the harshest of temptations and yet held fast. For when Jesus went into the wilderness and was tempted by the devil, it was in exactly these three areas that the devil tempted him: passions, ego, and will.

The Door of the Passions

It is no accident that at the start of his ministry Jesus went into the *wilderness*. He did not go there to get away from it all, as today we might go to a lakeside cabin with a backpack and a fishing rod. He went there deliberately to face down the Enemy. The wilderness was the place where Satan and his demons congregated. It was their convention center.

The Gospel of Matthew tells us very explicitly that "Jesus was led up by the Spirit into the wilderness to be tempted by the devil" (4:1). It was the start of a confrontation with the Enemy that would go all the way to the cross, and beyond—and would result in the devil being rendered ineffective.

So how did Satan begin to tempt Jesus? He began with the passions, the lust of the flesh:

> And after fasting forty days and forty nights, he was
> hungry. And the tempter came and said to him, "If you
> are the Son of God, command these stones to become
> loaves of bread" (Matthew 4:2-3).

You don't fast for forty days without working up an appetite. The prospect of bread must have been very appealing. As the Son of God, Jesus knew that his food was to do the will of his Father—obedience sustained him. But as the Son of man, he shared the weaknesses and needs of human flesh. When the devil came to him, he was ready to eat.

Notice how subtle the Enemy was. Not for a moment did Satan question Christ's divinity. Rather he treated it as a shared secret. He said, in effect, "Hey, you know and I know that you're God's Son. You could turn that stone into bread with a snap of your fingers, just by saying the word. Why not do it? What's stopping you?"

It seemed very reasonable. Jesus needed food. He had the power. The Father had given him the authority. He could raise the dead, perform healing miracles. Why not do this simple trick of supplying himself with a ready meal? What evil could possibly come of it? Surely this did not even qualify as a temptation—it was simply good sense.

But the evil was real. The issue here was not whether hunger should be satisfied, but whether a fast should be broken. Jesus had accepted the discipline of fasting for forty days. He knew the Father required this of him. To break the fast for the sake of satisfying his hunger, even hours before the allotted time was up, amounted to a serious breach of faith. It would have meant going back on his word.

In that sense this first temptation was exactly the same as the temptation to commit adultery. In themselves the appetites aren't wrong—sex and food are both God-given gifts. But both will become evils if indulging them involves breaking a prior commitment. Believers who are married have committed to their spouses, and believers who are single have committed to God. They are not free to indulge their sexual appetites at will.

Similarly, Jesus had made a commitment to the Father to abstain from food for the duration of his stay in the wilderness. He was not free to renegotiate the vow. The invitation to do so implied a challenge to God's authority. When Satan said, "If You are the Son of God…" he was suggesting to Jesus that his relationship with the Father was one of complete equality—that he had the right to break his vow if he wished.

Jesus had made a commitment to the Father to
abstain from food for the duration of his stay in the
wilderness. He was not free to renegotiate the vow.

Jesus, though, in spite of his equality, chose complete obedience to the Father. Though coequal to the Father as part of the Trinity, he was on earth to do his Father's will, not to challenge his authority. Obedience within the Godhead defined Jesus' place at the Father's right hand in glory. Rebellion and self-assertion could not have made him more God than he already is. He is fully God already. And had he been *less* than God, rebellion would not have improved his situation—as Satan well knew.

Many Christians make the mistake of thinking themselves limited by their commitments. They say, in effect, "I can't do that because God doesn't allow it." But notice how positively Jesus answered Satan. He did not say, "Bread isn't important, I don't need it," and he did not say, "Fasting is no fun but I've got to put up with it." Instead he simply put the appetites in the proper place—*below* the more important business of honoring vows and commitments. He also made clear that there is much, much more to life than satisfying your appetites:

> But he answered, "It is written,
>   'Man shall not live by bread alone,
>   but by every word that comes from the mouth
>   of God.'"
>   (Matthew 4:4)

The secret of Jesus' victory here is the secret of your victory and the secret of my victory. When Satan tries to tempt you down from the high ground by appealing to your passions, quote him the same Scripture Jesus used. When Satan comes to you appealing to the flesh, tell him that in Jesus you have been blessed with every spiritual blessing in the heavenly places, that in Jesus you have all of your sufficiency, and that you receive more nourishment from obedience to God than you do by indulging your passions.

The Door of the Ego

But Satan will not give up. If he cannot get in the first set of doors, he will try the second. He will move on from the passions to the ego.

He took Jesus into Jerusalem and stood with him on the roof of the temple. That was the highest place in the city—about four hundred feet above the Kidron Valley. From that vantage point the Enemy appealed to Jesus' ego:

> Then the devil took him to the holy city and set him on the pinnacle of the temple and said to him, "If you are the Son of God, throw yourself down, for it is written,
>
> 'He will command his angels concerning you,'
> and
> 'On their hands they will bear you up,
> lest you strike your foot against a stone.'"
> (Matthew 4:5-6)

Satan was not suggesting suicide. It was a clever tactical switch. He had figured out by now that he could not get to Jesus through the passions. Unlike Esau, who sold his birthright to his brother Isaac for a single plate of stew, Jesus would concede nothing even in the grip of a ravenous hunger. Seeing that this door was firmly closed, Satan beat a strategic retreat and rallied to attack on a different front.

"Okay," he said, "if I can't get to you through your passions, let me appeal to your ego. You say you believe the Word of God. Fine. Why don't you prove it? Throw yourself down."

At first it may be hard to see what Satan hoped to achieve. Throwing yourself off a building is not an idea most of us find attractive.

But see Jesus as Satan saw him: a poor man from the country, the son of a carpenter. Without learning, without a track record, and facing a people renowned for their dislike of prophets. To such a man, Satan reasoned, the prospect of beginning his ministry with a show-stopping, spectacular stunt must surely seem alluring.

And bear in mind that Jesus knew his Father would honor his scriptural promise. If Jesus had jumped, an angelic bodyguard would have flashed out of thin air and saved him. He would have gone from being a nobody to being an instant celebrity.

There is a lesson here. Do not let anyone tell you the devil is ignorant of Scripture. He knows it backward and forward. And he is very adept at producing a verse or two that appear to support his argument. So be wary of people who claim to have unearthed some radical new truth from the pages of the Bible. Look at what they are claiming the Bible says, and which of your instincts they are appealing to.

> Be wary of people who claim to have unearthed
> some radical new truth from the pages of the Bible.

You have heard people on television tell you, "Trust in Jesus and you'll become rich and happy." But where exactly does Scripture offer these apparently unconditional and cast-iron guarantees? Nowhere. And what motives are the preachers appealing to? Your selflessness and charity? Not likely. Being rich and happy is about as self-centered an ambition as you can have.

Note that no mention is made of the cross, of taking up the burden of good works, of sacrifice and martyrdom.

What we are looking at here is the lust of the eyes, the gospel of greed. It is Christianity without the cross. All you need to do, it says, is name that promise, whatever it is, and it will be yours. The emphasis is almost entirely on what you *want*. Anything you can see, God will get for you, as if God were Santa Claus. The only input from you is *naming and claiming*—oh, and swallowing whole a completely meaningless version of the Christian faith.

The advertising industry has got this down to a fine art. The advertisers know the connection between *perception* and *desire*. They know that if they display something for long enough and in the right way, you will end up wanting it.

You see a fifty-year-old woman on television who looks as if she's twenty—and you want the secret of her looks. You see a famous athlete wearing a particular brand of shoes, and you want those shoes. You see a successful man driving a certain kind of car, and you want that car. You see a person who is skinny as a rake eating low-fat yogurt, and you want that yogurt.

All of these images appeal to the lust of the eyes. All the advertisers have to do is pick the images they know we like and attach a product to them. Only occasionally does it backfire, as when a friend of mine told me that cottage cheese is fattening. "Every time I see a fat person," he said, "he's eating cottage cheese."

Do you spend time home shopping via the Internet? You are being asked to indulge in the lust of the eyes. All that matters to the advertiser is that you want the merchandise. He does not care whether you can afford it. He does not care whether you need it. He does not care if you're breaking a biblical principle by buying it. The product is shown to you with the specific aim of making you lust after it. The devil led Eve to do some home shopping when he showed her the tree of the knowledge of good and evil. And what did Eve do? What every home shopper does.

> So when the woman saw that the tree was good for food, and that it was a delight to the eyes, and that the tree was to be desired to make one wise, she took of its fruit and ate (Genesis 3:6).

Remember how, in Israel's invasion of the Promised Land and their defeat at Ai, Achan confessed,

> "Truly I have sinned against the LORD God of Israel, and this is what I did: when I saw among the spoil a beautiful cloak from Shinar, and 200 shekels of silver, and a bar of gold weighing 50 shekels, then I coveted them and took them. And see, they are hidden in the earth inside my tent, with the silver underneath" (Joshua 7:20-21).

Achan succumbed to the lust of the eyes. We desire things because we *see* them. We see, and soon we want to do more than just see: We want to *possess*. Ecclesiastes tells us that "the eye is not satisfied with seeing" (1:8), and Proverbs tells us that "never satisfied are the eyes of man" (27:20).

I remember the story about a spoiled little boy who always got everything he cried for. One day he was crying and crying and crying because he wanted an expensive vase that was sitting on a shelf, and the housekeeper wouldn't give it to him. The mother came over and said, "Why are you crying?"

He said, "I want that. I want that."

Unwisely—as some parents do, thinking the way to express love for their children is to give them everything they ask for—the mother reached out for that expensive vase and put it in front of the boy.

Did he stop crying? No, he cried even louder. His mother came back again and said, "What's wrong now?"

He kept on crying and said, "Oh, I want, I want—I want something I can't have!"

But back to the devil and his temptations. Satan had identified what he thought was a weak point in Jesus. After all, Jesus had come to earth in the form of a man. If he hoped to win anyone over to his cause, he would need to show that he was more than simply human. Why not take the easy route and announce his arrival with splashy headlines? People would join up as though they were going to a circus.

In addition, in order to be born among humankind as Mary's son, Jesus had taken a huge cut in salary and benefits. He must, the devil reasoned, have been missing the glory and worship and unquestioning obedience of the heavenly realm. If any sin would trip the Messiah, it was surely the sin of *coveting* fame and success.

Satan was wrong. Without hesitation,

> Jesus said to him, "Again it is written, 'You shall not put the Lord your God to the test'" (Matthew 4:7).

Which leaves us with a small problem. Clearly, Christian believers cannot rebuff the Enemy in quite the same way. We are not God, and Satan is within his rights to tempt us. We can, however, reject the temptation for the same *reason* Jesus did. For the fact is, anything Satan can offer us is already in our possession. Ambition, just like the appetites of hunger and sexual desire, can be felt in legitimate contexts and for pure motives. And after all, as Paul wrote to the Ephesians,

> But God, being rich in mercy, because of the great love with which he loved us, even when we were dead in our trespasses, made us alive together with Christ—by grace you have been saved—and raised us up with him and seated us with him in the heavenly places in Christ Jesus, so that in the coming ages he might show the immeasurable riches of his grace in kindness toward us in Christ Jesus (Ephesians 2:4-7).

Be careful, then, what you allow your eyes to see and your heart to desire. For nothing the Enemy offers can match what you have already been promised in Christ. To covet—to desire for selfish reasons something that others possess—is to be drawn down from the heights, made to fight the Enemy on level ground, and to suffer defeat.

> Be careful what you allow your eyes to see
> and your heart to desire. For nothing the
> Enemy offers can match what you have
> already been promised in Christ.

The Door of the Will

The lust of the flesh, said John, the lust of the eyes, and third, the pride of life. When Jesus would not allow Satan to come through the door of the passions or through the door of the ego, Satan tried a third entrance: the door of the will.

> Again, the devil took him to a very high mountain and showed him all the kingdoms of the world and their glory. And he said to him, "All these I will give you..." (Matthew 4:8-9).

This was another tactical switch. Jesus had not broken under the pressure of hunger. He had not broken before the lure of instant fame and success. So the devil tied his hanky to a stick and waved it. He made what appeared to be a critical concession.

Look at these verses carefully, because I want to explain something to you. When God the Creator made the world, he handed over the title deed to Adam. He said, "Adam, you're in charge. I'm giving you the scepter." And when Adam disobeyed God and fell for Satan's temptation, his fall sealed a coup. Satan had failed in his bid to take over heaven. But on earth he took command by subterfuge and stealth. He usurped the throne of the earth. That is why the Bible refers to Satan as "the god of this world." He rules it. It belongs to him. His demons have garrisoned the cities of earth and defend their borders.

Why are they doing this? Not simply to impose their rule, but because Satan knows his takeover is going to be challenged. It had always been God's purpose to wrest back the scepter from Satan's hand and give it to Jesus the Christ, the Son of man, who died on the cross and rose again—King of kings and Lord of lords.

When the Spirit drove Jesus out into the wilderness, Satan's intelligence networks had given him a pretty good idea of what was going on. They had examined the pages of the Old Testament. They had heard the prophet talking about men and women receiving new hearts, living under a new covenant with God. They knew a second David was coming. They knew the arrival of Jesus heralded the counterattack they had feared for so long. And now here were the two leaders, Jesus and Satan, face-to-face.

Satan offered the hand of friendship. He said, in effect, "All right. I know why you're here. I know you want to win back creation. I also know you are powerful. So why don't we settle this amicably? I'll return to you everything I have taken from God. Everything. It's all yours. I freely sign it over to you."

There is something strangely modern about this, isn't there? Can you see it? The attraction of the shortcut. Avoiding the conflict. Avoiding—in Jesus' case—the unpleasantness of crucifixion. The shortcut offers instant gratification without the cost. Satan was conceding to Jesus his entire program of salvation, his entire mission, victory in the whole cosmic conflict—on the easiest possible terms.

See how subtle this approach is? Satan was not asking Jesus to abuse his God-given passions or to covet someone else's property. By giving in to this third temptation, Jesus would, on the face of it, have been achieving what God wanted to achieve—the recovery of creation. There seemed to be every reason to say, "Yes, let's go make a deal."

But read the small print. For Satan attached one simple but devastating condition to his offer:

> And he said to him, "All these I will give you, if you will
> fall down and worship me" (Matthew 4:9).

In other words, Jesus could have had everything he wanted if only he would *submit his will to the devil.* Probably the devil would have allowed any number of miracles, healings, and good works. He would have permitted fellowship, unity among believers, even the preaching of the gospel—provided the whole enterprise remained under his own control and therefore separated from God.

Perhaps, had Jesus given in to this temptation, the church would have looked much the same as it does today. Except that the Enemy would own it, and eternal salvation would be only a mirage.

The Enemy will open up for you a way that
seems to fulfill the aims of God's kingdom,
asking in return only that you move away
from some area of clear biblical truth.

If the Enemy cannot ensnare you through the lust of the flesh or the lust of the eyes, he will use the pride of life. He will strike the most generous of bargains. He will offer to let you do tremendous good, open up for you a way that seems to fulfill the aims of God's kingdom, asking in return only that you move away from some area of clear biblical truth. We must be wary. Whenever a new strategy or idea is put before us, we must ask: *Will doing this keep me inside the will of God as revealed in Scripture—or will it move me outside it?*

Let me give you an example from my own church. Many years ago one dear brother was determined to change the way the church was run. He began to organize private meetings and hold behind-the-scenes discussions with some of the members of the leadership group. Around this time I became very ill and was unable to attend church meetings. As soon as I was out of circulation, this brother made his move. He had plenty of attractive arguments for moving the church in the direction he wanted it to go.

What he did not say was that the changes he wanted would alter the biblical direction of the church. A few members of the leadership group noticed this, but the brother gave them the impression that he had my full approval. Confusion resulted.

When I recovered and asked some of my friends how they could have allowed this brother to do what he did, their response was, "We thought you had a reason for it." But I had not even known what was going on. And I certainly would not have permitted the church to shift away from its biblical foundation. Needless to say, when I lovingly confronted the brother afterward, he decided to leave.

There is only one answer to the temptation to step outside the will of God as revealed in God's Word. It is the answer Jesus gave to Satan:

> Then Jesus said to him, "Be gone, Satan! For it is written,
> 'You shall worship the Lord your God
> and him only shall you serve.'"
> Then the devil left him, and behold, angels came and
> were ministering to him (Matthew 4:10-11).

STAY WHERE YOU CANNOT BE ATTACKED

Stay at high altitude. Stay on the high ground, where you have power over Satan and are sustained by the Word of God. In close combat, the Enemy seeks first to entice you down to his level, to open up one of the doors you should keep firmly shut. But if you remain spiritually in heavenly places with Christ, Satan cannot— yes, you read it right—Satan *cannot* attack you. You are out of his reach.

Stay on the high ground, where you have power
over Satan and are sustained by the Word of God

When somebody says to me, "I'm under attack," I say, "Let's examine your life. Where are you? Why is the Enemy attacking you? How has he drawn you down?"

These are the key questions. Because he could not be attacking you if you had not given him a way in. There is no transferring the blame. You either accept the attack, or you stop the attack and gain the victory when you get back to the high ground where you belong.

Please, please understand that by being attacked, I mean in those three areas only: lust of the flesh, lust of the eyes, and the pride of life. I don't mean attacked in the area of suffering when, like Job, you are in the very will of God.

There is a world of difference between test and temptation. I will say more about this later on. But here I am strictly speaking of temptation to sin, *not* the suffering for the sake of Christ that every serious believer must experience. In 2 Timothy 3:12 Paul assures us that "all who desire to live a godly life in Christ Jesus will be persecuted." This is not what I am talking about here.

Ask yourself what door or doors in your life you are leaving ajar for Satan. What door or doors do you fail to bolt every day? Some Christians think doors need closing only once, and after you have bolted the door, you can forget about it and you will automatically have the victory.

It's not true. Those doors have a habit of slipping open. Not because God is not faithful to his promises, but because it is up to us to make sure our obedience is continuous. Show me a Christian who falls again and again to the same sin, and I will show you a Christian who is not keeping an eye on the doors of his soul.

When I get up at five o'clock to pray, I am already bolting those doors mentally. I still have my eyes closed, I'm hardly awake, but I am imagining in my mind that I am turning the keys in the locks—keeping the Enemy out of my life and out of my family—standing in intercession with the doors bolted.

Do that every single day. You cannot afford to be lax. Do you want to be accessible to Satan's emissaries? Do you want to let in the demons that are constantly, whether you know it or not, roaring and prowling, looking for an opening to come in? Unless you deal with your open doors, Satan will steal your peace. Satan will rob you of your joy. Satan will destroy your relationships.

So anytime you feel temptation, ask yourself: *What is this appealing to? To my appetites? To my selfish nature? To my covetous nature? Or to my desire to go my own way instead of God's?* Every temptation falls into one of those three categories. And these are exactly the same categories through which Satan sought access to Jesus' life.

Success in any category will please him. But the last one, the capture of your will, is his ultimate prize. He wants us to give in to our appetites so regularly that we begin to rationalize sin as acceptable. To covet something so much that we begin to name that coveting as legitimate ambition. To go about the work of God in ways that put us outside the circle of biblical truth.

> Satan wants us to give in to our appetites so regularly
> that we begin to rationalize sin as acceptable.

These things are the Enemy's goal in combat because they drive the deepest wedge in your fellowship with your Savior. They put your commitment, your heart, your will, in a place other than God. They feed your self-centeredness and your pride. And they make you repeat the first sin of Adam and Eve—disregarding the Word of God and doing what *they* thought was best.

Occupy the high ground. Keep the doors bolted. There is no reason for you to be defeated. Satan may be a seasoned foe, strong and persistent and armed with deadly weapons, but he cannot touch you when you live in obedience to Christ.

And—as we will soon see—his days are numbered.

PART THREE

KNOW HOW TO
CONQUER THE ENEMY

CHAPTER 6

A SEVEN-POINT COUNTEROFFENSIVE

Throughout this book I have alluded to some of my own experiences in spiritual warfare. This is one of the hardest things for a pastor and a writer to do—indeed for anyone to do—to take a pair of binoculars and zoom in on his own weaknesses and show how God has dealt with them. It's threatening, but it's also good for me. Because it means I cannot hide behind these pages and pretend I am perfect, or that I have not suffered embarrassing defeats, or that as a minister I am somehow either immune to the kinds of attacks other Christians have to endure or singled out for attacks that are especially vicious. I am, in fact, exactly the same as you: a Christian called to fight against the devil and win.

So what's it like for me?

Let me give you one final example. One area where the Enemy knows he can get to me and rob me of my joy is false accusation. Being in ministry makes you responsible for many small and large decisions, and in all those decisions, the buck stops at your desk. In my case this is made slightly worse by the fact that I have strongly held opinions. As anyone who knows me will testify, my sense of God's calling is very clear. Details often do not bother me. I don't care whether the sanctuary is painted red or white, and it's not an issue who does the job, as long as the job gets done. But when it comes to the direction and the implementation of the ministry vision, I am emphatic.

Now here is the weakness. My shortcoming lies in dealing with the critical attitude of others. If I have reason to suspect that somebody else is critical of me, or of something I think, or of something I have done, I often find my finger on the trigger of a quick reply. Any questioning of my leadership in the important areas of ministry is apt to kindle my anger. I find it difficult to reason with my critics, or to explain quietly why I am taking a particular line, or what circumstances and convictions lie behind my decision.

I wish I *could*. I admire the more placid personalities who can reason things out. But that is not my character strength. Instead, I am far more likely to stew over some remark a person has made and to spend sleepless nights asking myself useless questions. *What does this person have against my preaching? How could he dare question my passion for evangelism? Doesn't he know me well enough not to question my motives?* And so on.

Let me be even franker with you. Along the way this tendency has led me into some errors. I have written some harsh letters that I wish I had never written. I have spoken some harsh words that I wish had never left my mouth. Even when I know in my heart of hearts that a rebuke was called for, I sometimes look back and realize that, given the chance again, I would have held my peace a little longer and been more measured in my words when I finally spoke.

> The good news is that the longer I walk in the
> Spirit the easier conquering becomes.

Many of you will identify with that. Others will be asking, "Why are you writing a book about overcoming the Enemy if you can't even handle your own problem? Why can't you find a way of dealing with this weakness of yours?"

Well, I have found a way. And I am dealing with it. I deal with it daily, and will continue to deal with it daily until I go to be with the Lord. I fight and, with God's help, win the match round by round—not with a knockout but on points. I bolt this door of impatience and anger, or any of my other weaknesses, by a seven-pronged plan of defense.

This tactic is not composed of quick one-two-three steps; some of them require thoughtful analysis and preparation. You may already know some of these seven points, but you need to remind yourself of these basic defense mechanisms each time the Enemy tempts you. The good news is that the longer I walk in the Spirit the easier conquering becomes.

1. REMEMBER, THE VICTORY IS OURS

Number one, I begin by remembering the theme of this book each day: The battle has already been fought, and the victory is ours. To remind myself that victory is assured, I need look no further than Scripture or any further back in the New Testament than the first book, the book of Matthew. Even before the resurrection, Jesus' arrival on earth had started to fray nerves in the Enemy's camp.

You can see it in the confrontation Matthew recorded between Jesus and the two demon-possessed men in the region of the Gadarenes. These men occupied the tombs. The demons had made these human beings so fierce, people were scared to go near them. Jesus had not been to this place before, and yet—significantly—the demons immediately recognized him and started to talk:

> And behold, they cried out, "What have you to do with us, O Son of God? Have you come here to torment us before the time?" (Matthew 8:29).

The word *torment* here means "consign to eternal punishment," something I'll look at further in the final chapter. You can always tell when discipline in an army is about to break down, because the troops stop thinking about victory and start thinking about survival.

These demons were doing just that. They recognized Jesus to be their judge. They recognized him as having authority over them. They sensed his power, and suddenly Satan's promises of glory and ascendancy over God looked hollow. It was no longer a question of whether they would be condemned; it was a question of *when*. They saw Jesus and the sulfurous reek of the lake of fire stung their nostrils, and they yelled out, "Have you come before we were expecting you?"

This was panic talking. They did not fight. They did not even threaten Jesus. Uppermost on their mind was saving their own skin. In fact, to keep the eternal flames at bay for a while longer, they were willing to contemplate almost any method of escape:

> Now a herd of many pigs was feeding at some distance from them. And the demons begged him, saying, "If you cast us out, send us away into the herd of pigs" (Matthew 8:30-31).

Jesus allowed this, so the confrontation ended with the undignified sight of these one-time angels thundering into the sea inside a herd of pigs. Not the kind of glorious victory Satan envisioned when he made his bid for the throne of heaven!

The story illustrates very well what James meant when he told believers: "Resist the devil, and he will flee from you" (James 4:7). Disarmed, the devil can do nothing to you. It's as if he has broken into your house and found you standing there, pointing a pistol at him. Not only is he helpless, he's scared. When you resist him, he recognizes the presence of Jesus in you—the same Jesus who outwitted him at the cross and who drove his minions into a herd of pigs—and all this once-glorious angelic being wants to do is turn on his heels and run.

> When you resist the devil, he recognizes the
> presence of Jesus in you and all this once-glorious
> angelic being wants to do is turn on his heels and run.

Are you this assertive with the devil? If so, why are so many Christians whining and wimping out instead of facing down the Enemy?

So Why Are We Whining?

It saddens me to say that many Christians never really resist Satan. Instead they go around with bowed shoulders and say, "You know, things are not going well. We've got to watch for this, and we've got to watch for that, and we've got to be careful." They are embattled, penned in, besieged. When they plant churches, they keep away from difficult neighborhoods because the territory is too dangerous. Instead of invading the Enemy's domain, they stay where they feel safe.

If they resist the devil at all, they do it so cautiously they might as well keep quiet. They say, "Oh devil, please don't do that. Just stay away from me." And then he comes up and gives them a shiny black eye, and they scurry back to God and say, "Well, Lord, you know I have a weak, fallen nature. I'm trying to resist him the best I can, but I just keep tripping up."

Now let me be straight with you. This is not resisting. This is wimping out spiritually. Did Paul end his letter to the Ephesians by saying: "Finally, my brethren, be wimps in the Lord"? No. He said,

> Finally, be strong in the Lord and in the strength of his might. Put on the whole armor of God, that you may be able to stand against the schemes of the devil (Ephesians 6:10-11).

Nowhere in the New Testament is it suggested that we should be retiring in our attitude toward the devil. Wimps get beaten to a pulp.

Paul called us to stand in the power of God's might. We cannot forget that Jesus rose victorious from the dead.

But what exactly happened on the cross?

Jesus Frees Us

I hesitate to write about this because the truth is so glorious it defies our powers of explanation. Though I have been walking with the Lord for over fifty years, I have never ceased to be amazed at the price God paid for my salvation, at what it cost Jesus to mount the counteroffensive into the Enemy's territory.

We think God's omnipotence made salvation straightforward, so we end up being blasé about what is the greatest miracle of all time: We have been received back into fellowship with God. Only in heaven will we even come close to understanding what it cost to make our redemption possible.

Read the words of Paul to the Colossians:

> And you, who were dead in your trespasses and the uncircumcision of your flesh, God made alive together with him, having forgiven us all our trespasses, by canceling the record of debt that stood against us with its legal demands. This he set aside, nailing it to the cross. He disarmed the rulers and authorities and put them to open shame, by triumphing over them in him (2:13-15).

The Enemy's greatest weapon against humankind is sin, because by getting us to sin, the Enemy draws us down from the heights and defeats us. Yet even in the worst of these skirmishes, he is unable to use his weaponry to full advantage because Jesus drained sin of its power. He disarmed the Enemy.

Jesus drained sin of its power. He
disarmed the Enemy.

To explain how this took place, Paul resorted to a very different image. His talk about nailing handwriting to the cross may seem obscure, but Paul was using language his readers readily understood: the language of the Roman law courts.

The Language of Roman Law

The first stage of a Roman prosecution was for the plaintiff to appear before the judge and present his case. He had to prove his testimony before the accused could even be brought to court. If the case reached the court, the plaintiff was again required to stand up and make his accusation—this time in the presence of the defendant as well as the judge.

Paul himself was indicted in this way. In Acts 24 you can read how the high priest Ananias and a hired orator named Tertullus accused Paul before the governor Felix, and how Paul defended himself against the charge. And elsewhere in the New Testament, when Timothy was called on to act as a judge between Christians, Paul advised him not to accept an accusation unless at least two other witnesses substantiated it (1 Timothy 5:19).

In the passage from Colossians, Paul uses the same picture of the Roman legal process to show how Jesus outwitted Satan at the cross. Satan is our accuser. Every day, almost hour by hour, he has been proclaiming the case against us. "Look at Michael Youssef," he says to the Father. "A pastor, and yet he can't turn the other cheek. Such anger!"

And make no mistake—the charges are serious and the proof plentiful. Satan has done his preparation. He knows the Word of God, and he knows the Bible says that the sinning soul shall die. He knows the Bible says that the wages of sin is death. So when Satan, the accuser, comes before God and denounces us for our sins, God, the judge, has to concede that these denunciations are just and true.

No one is righteous, says Scripture. Not one. Each of us has sinned and fallen short of the glory of God. The evidence is incontestable. Our telltale fingerprints are everywhere. We cannot deny the catalog of sins Satan brings against us. He did not have to hire some expensive private eye to go around the country searching for evidence. The evidence is staring him in the face!

Long before Satan even began his accusation, God knew we were guilty. He knew we were born in sin. He knew we would practice sin every day. And God, the judge, could not wink at sin, for he is a fair judge. To be otherwise would be to deny his nature. He could not listen to the accusation against us and then wave his hand and say, "Forget all that, it doesn't matter."

Sin *does* matter. All proved offenses matter. They demand judgment. And God cannot neglect to pass sentence any more than he can fail to determine guilt. Sometimes human courts fail; they condemn the innocent—as in the mockery of a trial that Jesus endured before Pontius Pilate—or they release the guilty. But these things cannot happen in God's court. For God is just. When Satan stands up in heaven and points his finger at you and me, no lawyer on earth or in heaven can get us off the hook.

I want to tell you, I have great respect for lawyers; my church is full of them. But God's law does not allow the same kind of disputation that human law allows. There are no extenuating circumstances. There is no possibility of plea bargaining. There are no loopholes or technicalities, no biased jurors.

We cannot claim any legal or political immunity. We cannot claim any protection on the basis of our intelligence or social background. We cannot defend ourselves by saying, "Well, you know, I was good here and good here and good here. I was bad only here." In God's law the rule is: One strike and you're out. We were guilty and—like Satan—we were all going down.

But blessed be his holy name! At that point, Jesus stepped in.

When a criminal was convicted under Roman law and a judge pronounced the sentence, a clerk of the court would be required to write down two things: the offender's crime and his sentence. When the jail guard took the offender to his cell, he nailed the paper bearing these two pieces of information to the door. If he had committed a capital crime—and in the Roman Empire, crucifixion was the usual sentence for such a crime—the guard would nail that same piece of paper to the offender's cross.

That is why Pontius Pilate wrote a notice on the cross of Jesus Christ: "Jesus of Nazareth, the King of the Jews" (John 19:19). Jesus was hanging there because he had been found guilty of a capital offense: treason.

But Pilate's sentence was not the only indictment nailed to the cross that day. Go back to Paul's letter to the Colossians.

> And you, who were dead in your trespasses and the uncircumcision of your flesh, God made alive together with [Christ], having forgiven us all our trespasses, by canceling the record of debt that stood against us with its legal demands. This he set aside, nailing it to the cross (2:13-14).

That set of *legal demands* was the indictment of sin against all those God has predestined to know him. It was a record of your iniquity and mine. It was a record of your disobedience and mine.

Jesus took upon himself the penalty for every sin you and I have committed or ever will commit.

But it no longer hangs on our cell door. God took it off and nailed it to the cross. Jesus took upon himself the penalty for every sin you and I have committed or ever will commit. He established the bridgehead and opened the way out of Enemy territory. Fully and comprehensively, he silenced every accusation Satan could make about God's elect and met the requirements of our sentence.

You can see this from the Gospel records of the Crucifixion.

The Last Moment on the Cross

John wrote that at the very end of Jesus' ordeal,

> Jesus, knowing that all was now finished, said (to fulfill the Scripture), "I thirst." A jar full of sour wine stood there, so they put a sponge full of the sour wine on a hyssop branch and held it to his mouth. When Jesus had received the sour wine, he said, "It is finished," and he bowed his head and gave up his spirit (John 19:28-30).

The Greek word translated "It is finished!" is *tetelestai*. It is no coincidence that this word also has a legal connotation. Roman law was meant to be scrupulously fair. When a prisoner had served his term in detention, or—as happened occasionally—if he had been pardoned, his jailers would release him and take him back to court, along with the piece of paper that was nailed to his cell door. The prisoner would see the same judge who sentenced him, and that judge would take a pen and write across the page one word: *tetelestai*. Paid in full. The piece of paper that once had borne witness to the bearer's guilt and shame now bore witness to his right to freedom. He had paid his debt. It was finished. Nobody could send him back to prison unless he committed another offense.

Consequently, the freed criminal would often take that piece of paper back home with him and nail it to the front door of his house. If any of his old enemies came by and said, "What is that fellow doing out of prison?" the freed man could point to the paper and to that one word, *tetelestai*. He could say, "You have no claim over me. I am a free man. My debt is paid in full." His safety, his liberty, and his future depended on that one word, *tetelestai*.

And that is exactly the word Jesus used in his last moment on the cross. Notice how Jesus was in control at Calvary. Most people who were nailed to a cross simply hung there and waited to die. Not Jesus.

> When Jesus had received the sour wine, he said, "It is finished," and he bowed his head and gave up his spirit (John 19:30).

His life was not taken away from him; he laid it down. And the last thing he did before he allowed his spirit to depart from his body was to utter the cry of victory: *"Tetelestai!"* Not, "Thank goodness it's over." But, "The price is paid in full. Satan is defeated!"

That, I suspect, was the moment Satan first realized he had been outwitted. He had actively pursued the Crucifixion, thinking perhaps that killing Jesus would frustrate God's plans. He even entered into the heart of Judas Iscariot in order to make it possible. He did not know that he was playing into God's hands by engineering the death of Jesus, that by inflicting what he thought was a crushing defeat he had unintentionally conceded the decisive battle of the counteroffensive. For that word, *tetelestai*, suddenly and drastically curtailed the Enemy's power.

> Satan did not know that he was playing into God's hands by engineering the death of Jesus.

Until that point he had been able to use God's judgment as a weapon. He could say of anyone on earth, "He's mine, she's mine," because God cannot look on the face of sin. But now—to his surprise—there were people over whom he had no power, people whose numbers began growing as the kingdom spread.

The Enemy lost his power. In Paul's words, Jesus "disarmed the rulers and authorities and put them to open shame, by triumphing over them in him" (Colossians 2:15). If you have committed your life to Jesus Christ, if Jesus is your only Savior and Lord, then Satan has no legal right over you. No legal right to trespass on your property. No legal right to harass you. No legal right to come into your life when he wants to and leave when he wants to.

You do not belong to him anymore. When Jesus said, *"Tetelestai!"* you became a free man, a free woman. At that very instant, locks were installed on the inside of your soul's doors. You could shut the Enemy out. And once those doors have been locked and bolted, there is no reason on earth why you need to have the Enemy trampling over your life and defeating you.

So the first way I bolt the door of impatience and anger is to remember that the battle has been won. I do not have to justify myself. Jesus did it for me. I say to Satan, *"Tetelestai!* It is finished." And I remind myself: "Christ died for you, Michael. Surely you can overcome your anger."

To do that I must also overcome my need to retaliate. And I can do that only if I lay down my life to Jesus in each instance, so that I no longer care what other people think.

2. THE SECRET OF MASADA: LAY DOWN YOUR LIFE

At the southwestern edge of the Dead Sea is a mountaintop fortress called Masada. The rocky cliffs rise 1,300 feet above the surrounding desert, and on the top of it lie the remains of a military encampment. Masada holds a special place in the memory of the Jewish people, for it was at Masada that Israel's conflict with Rome reached its climax.

In the century after Jesus came, Jewish relations with Rome broke down into a rebellion, which the Romans ruthlessly put down. And the last band of rebels—just 930 men, women, and children—retreated to the fortress atop the rocky peak of Masada.

Standing on top of the towering cliffs, those persecuted people could see the outline of the Roman military camp below. But the rock was almost unscalable, affording the Jewish rebels a secure refuge for several years. Eventually the Romans built a vast dirt ramp—some 200 feet high and 645 feet long—to besiege the stronghold; the remains are still visible today. Once the mighty Roman soldiers finally scaled the walls of the fortress, however, they met no resistance. Every one of the 930 men, women, and children lay dead. They had killed themselves rather than face the indignity of death or enslavement at the hands of the Romans.

So powerful is the memory of that event that every modern Israeli soldier is taken to Masada for a swearing-in ceremony. With history ringing in their ears, they swear never again to let Israel be brought into bondage.

Christians should take note of this. Our invisible war against the Enemy is every bit as serious as the Jewish war against Rome. And like those 930 Jews at Masada, we are called to lay down our lives. Please don't think for a moment that I am advocating suicide (like Jonestown or Heaven's Gate) or martyrdom or even valor on the field of battle. I simply mean that in spiritual terms we must learn to die to ourselves in order to live in victory, for that is the secret of staying on the high ground where Satan cannot reach us.

> In spiritual terms we must learn to die to ourselves in order to live in victory, for that is the secret of staying on the high ground where Satan cannot reach us.

Go back to the verse I quoted earlier in this chapter from James. In fact I only gave you the second part of the verse. The full version goes like this:

> Submit yourselves therefore to God. Resist the devil, and he will flee from you (4:7).

The connection of these two thoughts is no accident. Successful resisting flows from successful submitting. What is most terrifying to the Enemy is the life that is totally dedicated to God in every

detail, because this person's heart is ironclad, completely impene-
trable to the Enemy's weapons.

Someone asked George Mueller, the great man of faith of the
nineteenth century (and one of my heroes), "What is the secret of
your victorious Christian living?"

"It was the day I died, utterly died," Mueller said. Then he leaned
over, literally touching the ground, as he went on, "Died to George
Mueller, to his opinions, to his preferences, to his tastes, to his will.
I died to the world, to its approval or censure. Died to the approval
or blame even of my brethren and my friends. And since I have done
this, I have studied only to show myself approved unto God."

Mueller lived out what Paul the apostle taught in Romans:

> We know that our old self was crucified with him in
> order that the body of sin might be brought to noth-
> ing, so that we would no longer be enslaved to sin. For
> one who has died has been set free from sin. Now if we
> have died with Christ, we believe that we will also live
> with him. We know that Christ, being raised from the
> dead, will never die again; death no longer has domin-
> ion over him. For the death he died he died to sin, once
> for all, but the life he lives he lives to God. So you also
> must consider yourselves dead to sin and alive to God in
> Christ Jesus (6:6-11).

The old man has died; the new man has been resurrected. Submitting to God, therefore, can be thought of as keeping the old man
dying daily. Again, in Paul's words,

> Let not sin therefore reign in your mortal body, to
> make you obey its passions. Do not present your mem-
> bers to sin as instruments for unrighteousness, but pre-
> sent yourselves to God as those who have been brought
> from death to life, and your members to God as instru-
> ments for righteousness. For sin will have no dominion

over you, since you are not under law but under grace (6:12-14).

We need to surrender in total obedience, without hesitation and without reservation. That is the secret of making the devil flee.

When I am falsely accused, I do not need to retaliate even if I am innocent—because I am no longer seeking this person's approval, or anyone else's. I only seek my Father's approval. And I have to tell myself that each time I become angry.

Remember, the victory is ours. Remember the secret of Masada: lay down your life. And third, remember to lock the doors to your soul each morning.

3. LOCK THE DOORS EACH MORNING

I mentioned this previously, but it is so important we need to see it here again as part of our battle plan.

Every morning as I wake up I bolt the doors of my heart that are susceptible to sin. I begin by bolting the gate of the city—every area of my life. The moment I claim I have certain areas of strength— "This area is really fine"—that is the downfall for me. Pride was the devil's sin; it can also be mine.

> Every morning as I wake up I bolt the doors
> of my heart that are susceptible to sin.

So I begin by praying for strength in every area: greed, lust, pride. Then I go to the smaller doors, like anger and impatience with people.

The devil cannot defeat us unless we get sloppy and start leaving those doors unlocked. That is the reality for many believers. They are too busy; they miss their quiet time; they get distracted. And sooner or later they discover they have been drawn down from the high places of fellowship with God and are once again taking a knockout from the devil. They feel trapped, as if becoming a Christian has made no difference, as if all their efforts to live a Christian life can achieve no more than a monotonous cycle of failure and guilt.

Is that your spiritual reality? If so, take careful note—because Satan has you hoodwinked.

So often, even in the evangelical church, Christians attend worship Sunday by Sunday, listening to the gospel message but going no further. They get saved on Sunday, but never learn how to live in the power and victory of Christ for the rest of the week. Christ does not lead us in triumphal procession on Sundays only, however. He leads us on Mondays and Tuesdays and Wednesdays and Thursdays and Fridays and Saturdays. Paul pictured us as constantly returning from the war, as the Roman generals did, in a garland-strewn victory parade, marching behind our Leader in his strength.

> But thanks be to God, who in Christ always leads us in triumphal procession, and through us spreads the fragrance of the knowledge of him everywhere (2 Corinthians 2:14).

We are called not only to stop the Enemy from getting into our lives, but actually to drive him away from us. Not only to go around bolting the doors of our soul against Satan, the prowling lion, but to use our own lethal weaponry in such a way that the Enemy flees in terror.

And that means that as Christians we have to undergo a training course of the most demanding kind. Let's turn now and look at those next steps—steps that will keep the Enemy on the run.

CHAPTER 7

KEEPING THE ENEMY ON THE RUN

Every time I preach or write, it is not just a matter of getting
up and throwing some Scripture together. My sermons grow
out of prayer, and in much of that prayer I find myself on my
knees, going into hand-to-hand combat with the devil.

The next step in my seven-point counteroffensive against the
Enemy is what Paul taught in Ephesians 6 about wrestling against
principalities and powers. Every soldier needs to put on his battle
gear, whether it be khaki fatigues or old-fashioned armor.

4. PUT ON YOUR BATTLE GEAR

I have quoted from Ephesians 6 already because that is where
Paul warned Christians they do not wrestle against flesh and blood,
but against the fourfold infernal hierarchy, the Enemy's chain of
command. Immediately after Paul's description of the Enemy's
forces, he continued with this advice to believers:

> Therefore take up the whole armor of God, that you may
> be able to withstand in the evil day, and having done all,
> to stand firm (6:13).

Much has been written and preached on the verses that follow. But I believe this armor of God is of three types: the uniform, the defensive weapons, and the offensive weapons.

The Uniform

Paul went on,

> Stand therefore, having fastened on the belt of truth, and having put on the breastplate of righteousness, and, as shoes for your feet, having put on the readiness given by the gospel of peace (6:14-15).

I don't want to push Paul's analogy too far, but these items constitute a Christian's basic survival kit—the equipment and clothing that identify his necessary attributes and enable him to go where his Commander directs. Jesus' own life was characterized by this same triad: truth, righteousness, and gospel peace. Answering his Jewish critics, Jesus said,

> "He who speaks from himself seeks his own glory; but He who seeks the glory of the One who sent Him is true, and no unrighteousness is in Him" (John 7:18 NKJV).

Truth and righteousness belong together. Yet they are not static. They have a purpose, and that purpose, in Jesus and now in his followers, is proclaiming the gospel.

Look again at that incident where Jesus asked who the disciples thought he was. Peter replied, almost without thinking, "You are the Christ, the Son of the living God" (Matthew 16:16). Nobody had told him that. As Jesus said, "flesh and blood has not revealed this to you, but my Father who is in heaven" (16:17).

At this stage Peter had no idea that truth and righteousness had some other purpose outside of themselves. That was why, not long afterward, he reacted so badly when Jesus shared what he had come to earth to do:

> From that time Jesus began to show his disciples that he
> must go to Jerusalem and suffer many things from the
> elders and chief priests and scribes, and be killed, and on
> the third day be raised. And Peter took him aside and
> began to rebuke him, saying, "Far be it from you, Lord!
> This shall never happen to you" (Matthew 16:21-22).

Peter disliked change. But that was what the gospel demanded, so Jesus began to break the news. In effect he took the disciples aside and said, "Now, men, I want to tell you something. I'm going to die on the cross, because that's what I have to do in order to redeem you from sin and save you eternally. I'm telling you this now because pretty soon it will be your job to tell the world. Now being true and righteous is one thing. Letting that truth and righteousness spill out in the form of the good news is quite another. The first is static and safe. The second puts you out on the open ocean. It is challenging, demanding."

And that's when Peter got scared, just as he got scared when he climbed out of the boat to walk on the water with Jesus and then saw the huge waves below him.

Today's counselors would have treated Peter with kid gloves. They would have said, "He needs time to adjust, he needs stress management, he needs therapy."

Jesus got right to the core of the issue. He said to Peter,

> "Get behind me, Satan! You are a hindrance to me. For
> you are not setting your mind on the things of God, but
> on the things of man" (16:23).

This was not willfully riding roughshod over Peter's feelings. The preaching of the gospel was just so crucial, nothing but a truthful approach would do.

The principle Jesus implied here still stands. Every time you get out of the will of God, you are doing Satan's bidding. There is no territory in the invisible war that is neutral or undisputed. Every area of your life is under the control of either God or the devil. Consequently, even the best reasons for drawing back from God's work are, ultimately, satanically inspired.

> Every time you get out of the will of God,
> you are doing Satan's bidding.

Every time you let your pride get in the way, every time you shrink back from sharing the gospel and doing what you know God wants you to do, Satan is using you. Every time you refuse to resist the devil, refuse to send him packing, you have bought into Satan's lie. By contrast, every time you stand firm in truth and righteousness, you put the Enemy to flight.

Challenges will come every day. When God calls on you to make some really big sacrifice, someone will say, "That doesn't make sense. Don't do it. Let somebody else do it." God calls you to full-time ministry, and others say, "Don't do such a thing. Let others do it." God calls you to take a job that pays less than you think you deserve. You take something below your level, and God says, "Do it because I want to use you in a certain way." And somebody else says, "No, don't do such a thing. Go for the gold."

Sometimes we get it wrong. But, like Peter, we do not have to be burdened by our failures.

What do you do when your shoe comes untied? You stoop down and tie it. What do you do if your belt falls loose? You buckle it up again. Similarly, if you're wearing a breastplate, you don't put it down the moment one of the straps falls off. You refasten it. The Christian life is like driving on the highway. If a tire blows, you don't abandon the car. You put on the spare and get back on the road.

One of the reasons Peter is such a great encouragement to me is that he fell so badly, so many times. Yet he never stayed down! He knew how to accept God's forgiveness and start again. So by the time he wrote his epistles, he spoke from a wealth of experience. When I read those words of Peter's I quoted earlier—"Be sober-minded; be watchful. Your adversary the devil prowls around like a roaring lion, seeking someone to devour" (1 Peter 5:8)—I know Peter experienced this firsthand.

When Satan tempts me to retaliate, I put on my battle fatigues, my uniform of truth and righteousness. I must turn the other cheek, for the Scripture, God's truth, says so. Then, when I am dressed for combat, I gather together my defensive weapons.

Defensive Weapons

Paul next outlined two pieces of battle gear each soldier must have for protection:

> In all circumstances take up the shield of faith, with which you can extinguish all the flaming darts of the evil one; and take the helmet of salvation (Ephesians 6:16-17).

Do you remember when the people of Israel were living in slavery in Egypt, and Pharaoh refused to let them go—even after nine plagues? Probably the Israelites' confidence in Moses and Aaron hit an all-time low. And yet the next thing they heard from Moses was this:

> "Go and select lambs for yourselves according to your clans, and kill the Passover lamb. Take a bunch of hyssop and dip it in the blood that is in the basin, and touch the lintel and the two doorposts with the blood that is in the basin. None of you shall go out of the door of his house until the morning" (Exodus 12:21-22).

Painting your door with blood did not sound quite as strange to the Israelites as it does to us today. Nevertheless, it must have been tempting for them to say, "O God, we are suffering here in slavery in Egypt. How is it going to help us to put blood on our doors?"

Or everybody could have gotten together and said, "Let's vote on this." But no—they just obeyed. They did not understand what God had in mind, but they obeyed anyway. They painted blood over the door frames and went to sleep. In the middle of that night, as God went through the land of Egypt slaying the firstborn, every time he came to a house marked faithfully with the blood, he saw it and passed over that house.

> God himself has declared that whoever
> is marked with the blood of Jesus shall
> stand beyond the reach of the devil.

There is a truth in that passage from Exodus, a truth that applies directly to us. Like the Israelites, the only thing separating us from destruction is blood—the blood of Jesus. His blood protects us completely. Once we are marked with the blood we cannot be touched—by God's judgment or by the devil. Because the blood says, "Pass over, do not harm." No power in hell can get past that blood, because it is a seal established on the authority of God and God's Word.

God himself has declared that whoever is marked with the blood of Jesus shall stand beyond the reach of the devil. The blood-washed person will be taken into God's territory, into the bridgehead of God's kingdom. The price has been paid for his salvation, that word *tetelestai* striking out the record of his sins.

So remember: You may be assaulted by the Enemy in all kinds of ways. He may come at you through the doors of sin. He may come at you through your emotions. He may come at you through your mental state and feelings of oppression and depression. He may come at you through overwork, stressed relationships, a cooling of your love for Jesus Christ. But whatever route the Enemy takes, no matter how frightening and invincible he looks, the moment you plead the blood of Jesus he will begin to turn and run away from you.

This is not because of anything you are or anything you have done. It does not matter what your net worth is, or what family you come from. It does not matter if you are Episcopalian or Presbyterian or Baptist or Pentecostal. It does not matter how long you have been a Christian. It does not matter whether you find the life of faith easy or hard. Your victory is not based on any of that. Your victory is based on the death and resurrection of the Lord Jesus Christ. His death on the cross not only provided your salvation, but it has armed you against the Enemy's onslaught. It is your shield and your helmet.

And this grace of God is given to us day in and day out. It is not something that happened in the past, when you gave your life to Christ and became born again. It is given to you afresh every morning, every hour. God did not call us to hide from the Enemy. God did not call us to outsmart the Enemy by our own resources. No! God called us to plead the blood of his Son, Jesus, to defend ourselves with the helmet of salvation and the shield of faith. He called us to withstand actively, believing the Word of God and what it says about our authority and victory in Jesus Christ, and about putting the Enemy, the wicked one, to flight.

We have been thoroughly equipped to withstand the Enemy's attack. We have the uniform of truth and righteousness. We have defensive weapons of a shield and a helmet—the blood of Jesus. And we have offensive weapons to put Satan on the run.

We have been thoroughly equipped
to withstand the Enemy's attack.

Offensive Weapons

Finally Paul says, "and take...the sword of the Spirit, which is the word of God" (Ephesians 6:17).

Jesus used the sword of the Spirit against the Enemy in the wilderness. In reply to the devil's suggestions and insinuations, Jesus simply quoted the eternal, infallible, indisputable, and unambiguous Word of God. It works like the ace of trumps. There is no answer to the Word. No way around it, no way beyond it. It marks the end of the argument.

It is the *sword* of the Spirit, and that is exactly how you use it—you pick up your sword and go on the offensive. You might make a slight adjustment for the sake of helping your imagination by bringing the technology up to date. Had Paul been writing in the twenty-first century, perhaps he would have called God's Word an Uzi or a semiautomatic.

So how do you use your offensive weapons? Say the Enemy comes to you, through one of his demons or through some other person, and brings doubt to your heart about your Christian walk. He whispers, "Are you really a Christian? Do you really think you're going to heaven?" You pull out the big gun of 1 John 5:11-12, and you say to him: "And this is the testimony, that God gave us eternal life, and this life is in his Son. Whoever has the Son has life; whoever does not have the Son of God does not have life."

Or the Enemy comes to you and whispers, "Your sins are too big for God to forgive. You've done so many miserable things in the past, God could never forgive you." Here's what you do. You pull out 1 John 1:9 and say to him, "If we confess our sins, he is faithful and just to forgive us our sins and to cleanse us from all unrighteousness."

Or the Enemy comes to you and taunts, "Look at your miserable condition! You're not even able to get up from your bed. You can't even shake depression. You're a wreck. How can you say that God loves you?" Here's what you do. You blow him away with Romans 5:8: "but God shows his love for us in that while we were still sinners, Christ died for us."

Or the Enemy comes to you and says, "God doesn't answer prayer these days. If God answered prayer, you'd be out of this mess.

Look how long you've been waiting." Here's what you do. You run him through with John 16:24: "Until now you have asked nothing in my name. Ask, and you will receive, that your joy may be full."

Or the Enemy tries to hit you through suffering—physical suffering, financial suffering, whatever trying circumstances you are facing. Throw 2 Corinthians 12:9 at him: "But [Jesus] said to me, 'My grace is sufficient for you, for my power is made perfect in weakness.' Therefore I will boast all the more gladly of my weaknesses, so that the power of Christ may rest upon me."

Or the Enemy says to you, as he does to me, "You've been wronged. You've been falsely accused. You have reason to be angry." Here's what you do. You stab his logic with Proverbs 16:32: "Whoever is slow to anger is better than the mighty, and he who rules his spirit than he who takes a city."

When the Enemy tries to knock me out, I remember the victory is ours. I remember the secret of Masada: lay down your life. I lock the doors of my soul each morning. I put on my battle gear. And then I begin praising the Lord.

5. PRAISE THE LORD

Several years ago I heard a story about an elderly gentleman who was at a midweek prayer meeting. He began his prayer by saying, "O Lord, we will praise you, we will praise you with an instrument of ten strings!"

Well said, don't you think? You see, praise is total; it is praise of the mind and praise of the heart, as well as praise of the lips.

When you think about it, that's exactly what the angels are doing all the time in heaven. And that's what other Christians who have gone before us are also doing in heaven. They are continuously worshiping God and praising God and adoring God.

And that is what you and I will be doing when we close our eyes and go home to be in the presence of God.

Now, what does all this have to do with victory over the Enemy?

When I am angry at someone who has falsely accused me, the spiritual realm becomes misty, foggy, unreal. I begin to think that the world I can see is the real world, which is what Madison Avenue and the media are trying to convince me of.

Yet the truth of Scripture is this: What we call "the real world," this fallen, tangible world, is not ultimate reality. What is ultimately real is the invisible realm, the spiritual realm, the realm in the presence of God. And when I praise him, I enter into that heavenly realm.

Praise changes the atmosphere of my anger and bitterness. Praise changes my attitude toward the person who has falsely accused me. Regardless of my circumstances, no matter how difficult they may be, if I begin to praise God I will be uplifted.

> Regardless of my circumstances, no matter how difficult they may be, if I begin to praise God I will be uplifted.

Remember that the next time you have an argument with your spouse. Start singing praises, and if you can't sing, download some worship music for your home and your car. Just praise God.

The devil's hordes are everywhere. When you get out of church, they are sitting in the car, waiting for you, ready to steal your joy and your blessing. That's when the Enemy does his best work, getting people to argue with one another. The way to stop him is to start praising God—and Satan will flee in a minute.

You see, God is specifically present in the praises of his people. And his power is especially manifested in our praises.

Henry W. Frost, a veteran missionary to China, had a great impact on that nation. However, his ministry was not effective until he discovered the incredible lesson of praising God. In his autobiography he writes, "Nothing so pleases God in connection with our prayer as praise...and nothing so blesses the man who prays as the praise which he offers."

Frost then goes on to tell what happened one day when he received sad news from home. "A deep shadow had covered my soul, I prayed and I prayed, but the darkness didn't vanish. I summoned myself to endure, but the darkness only deepened.

"Then I went to an inland station and saw on the wall of the mission home these words: 'Try praising the Lord.' I did, and in a moment every shadow was gone, not to return. Yes, the psalmist was right, it is a good thing to give praise unto the Lord."

> "Yes, the psalmist was right, it is a good
> thing to give praise unto the Lord."

In order to praise God properly, we must remember one of the names of God: *El Shaddai*, which was understood by God's people as "God Almighty" or "God of all power" or "God who is all sufficient."

El Shaddai means that God intervenes on behalf of his people. *El Shaddai* brought the Israelites out of Egypt.

El Shaddai alone can

- sustain you
- protect you
- redeem you

El Shaddai will protect me when someone falsely accuses me. As I praise God, I turn the situation over to his power and he helps me overcome my anger.

And then I begin to pray for the person who has angered me.

6. PRAY FOR THE OTHER PERSON

If there is even a grain of truth in what my critic has said about me, I try (I don't need to tell you how hard this is!) to receive it in an attitude of humility. You'll remember that John once responded to Jesus' critics by asking if he should call fire down from heaven to consume them. Most of the time that is very tempting, because it satisfies our craving for revenge.

But that is not what I mean by praying for someone. I mean praying for a person by name. Praying for his business, his wife, and his children. Praying for his well-being. In doing so I find I override my natural instincts. I erase my "default setting" and impose a new behavior on myself. And in my case this is very effective. By doing good to a person who has hurt me, I immediately begin to feel the victory.

Before I mention the final counteroffensive against the Enemy, let's review the first six:

1. Remember, the victory is ours.

2. Remember the secret of Masada: lay down your life.

3. Lock the doors of your soul each morning.

4. Put on your battle gear.

5. Praise the Lord.

6. Pray for the other person.

7. START THINKING OF HEAVEN

By this time my critic and I will be in fellowship with each other, and each of us will see the other as God sees us. In other words, I deliberately take myself out of my current time frame. I refuse to see my present situation as enduring or unchangeable. I force myself to look through present imperfection to a future where I am more fully reconciled than I can ever be on earth.

By these means I lock the devil out. I never begin by indulging or even consulting my feelings. I know well enough how I *feel* about a person who has accused me. It's my feelings that are causing the problem. So I move away from my feelings of anger and turn my attention to the eternal truth of God—something stronger than my feelings, and something that is capable of bringing my feelings into line.

I know the devil is defeated when I can emerge from this process, meet my critic, and give him a warm—and completely genuine—hug. That does not mean he won't lash out at me again, and that I won't be challenged by my impatience all over again in the future. But that day's battle has been fought and won.

I think it was Lord Nelson who overwhelmed the French at the Battle of the Nile and then reported the event to the British Admiralty by writing, "Victory is not a large enough word to describe what has taken place in that battle." British understatement, no doubt.

But when you resist the devil, and he flees from you as the Bible promised he would, the whole of heaven is watching and cheering for you. Even in the smallest things, *victory* is not a large enough word to describe what has taken place.

CHAPTER 8

THE ENEMY'S FUTURE

The Enemy is at work everywhere in our culture. And as Christians we find ourselves constantly at war with him. If that is *not* your experience of the Christian life, then something is wrong. Spiritually, you live in a war zone. You cannot be neutral; you cannot avoid taking sides. If you are not fighting on the side of Christ, you are open to the devil. And if you have escaped from the Enemy's clutches and crossed into God's territory, then you are enlisted, and the devil is after you.

Beware of the easy life. Christianity should not be a pleasant cycle of church events: services, Bible studies, coffee mornings, elders' meetings. It's true that if you have closed all the doors of your soul to Satan, you occupy the high ground and he cannot touch you. But if Satan isn't *trying* to attack you, there is something amiss with your Christian walk. You are not stirring him up. You are not making him mad enough. You are not ruffling his feathers. When I go for a day without a head-on collision with Satan, I'm worried. It could mean I'm doing something he likes.

Know your enemy. By now you should know him pretty well. In the past chapters we've looked at every area of his organization and strategy. We have learned about his chain of command. We have learned about his deceptive character. We have discovered how he tries to keep Christians weak and ineffective. We have found out how he uses the doors of the passions, the ego, and the will to get into your life and manipulate you. We have also learned how Satan was completely defeated at the cross, and how we should apply that victory to our own lives by keeping the devil on the run.

Everyone on the devil's side realizes his time will soon be up, that the invisible war is racing to its conclusion. And so I want to use the final chapter of this book to give you an insight into the Bible's teaching on the future—what the Enemy and his minions' end will be, and what God promises to his soldiers.

SENTENCE PASSED ON SATAN

The Bible teaches us that immediately before the return of Christ there is going to be a tidal wave of rebellion and sin across the world. It will sweep the entire planet because the devil and his fallen angels know they are about to be overthrown. Revelation 20:7-15 describes this final rebellion:

> And when the thousand years are ended, Satan will be released from his prison and will come out to deceive the nations that are at the four corners of the earth, Gog and Magog, to gather them for battle; their number is like the sand of the sea. And they marched up over the broad plain of the earth and surrounded the camp of the saints and the beloved city, but fire came down from heaven and consumed them, and the devil who had deceived them was thrown into the lake of fire and sulfur where the beast and the false prophet were, and they will be tormented day and night forever and ever.
>
> Then I saw a great white throne and him who was seated on it. From his presence earth and sky fled away, and no place was found for them. And I saw the dead, great and small, standing before the throne, and books were opened. Then another book was opened, which is

the book of life. And the dead were judged by what was written in the books, according to what they had done. And the sea gave up the dead who were in it, Death and Hades gave up the dead who were in them, and they were judged, each one of them, according to what they had done. Then Death and Hades were thrown into the lake of fire. This is the second death, the lake of fire. And if anyone's name was not found written in the book of life, he was thrown into the lake of fire.

The terms *Gog* and *Magog* are symbolic figures representing the nations of the world that band together for the final assault upon God and his people. They are simply hostile nations from all across the world. These nations have no lasting power. Notice that God supernaturally, miraculously, and powerfully intervenes on behalf of his children, and he will save them from the fire that will engulf their enemies.

But you will notice that the devil doesn't get consumed by the fire from heaven, but rather he is thrown into the lake of fire to be tormented day and night, forever and ever.

Isn't that great! The great deceiver who deceives kids into using drugs, who deceives husbands and wives into destroying their marriages, who deceives people into thinking they don't need God, who deceives people into believing that God doesn't love them, who deceives people into lying and cheating and cursing, who deceives people into stealing and murdering and destroying other people's reputations—he and all of his, will be thrown into the lake of fire.

But how do we know this will happen?

When he died and rose again, Jesus pronounced Satan's sentence—and he will carry out that sentence when he returns.

When he died and rose again, Jesus pronounced Satan's sentence—and he will carry out that sentence when he returns. Look at John 12, where Jesus was preparing himself for the events that would lead to his death. Some Greeks who had come to Jerusalem for the Passover celebration told the disciples that they wanted to meet Jesus, and so Philip and Andrew came to Jesus to pass along their request:

> And Jesus answered them, "The hour has come for the Son of Man to be glorified. Truly, truly, I say to you, unless a grain of wheat falls into the earth and dies, it remains alone; but if it dies, it bears much fruit" (12:23-24).

Jesus spoke of his death as the hour when "the Son of Man" would "be glorified"—not the obvious way to describe dying. Further, he said that his death would not be the end, but would result in a greater and glorious multiplication of life, like the death of a grain of wheat. Shortly afterward he was even more explicit:

> "Now is the judgment of this world; now will the ruler of this world be cast out. And I, when I am lifted up from the earth, will draw all people to myself" (12:31-32).

Jesus said, "Satan's rule is about to finish. He thinks that by crucifying me he will frustrate God's plan for creation, but the reverse will happen. As I am raised up on the cross, I will draw to myself believers from among all of humanity." The Lord Jesus Christ condemned Satan, and now it is only a matter of time before Christ completes the work he started on the cross. He is going to execute judgment on Satan and all of his demons. Not one of them is going to escape. The power of God will carry them away like flotsam on the incoming tide.

By the end of his earthly ministry, Jesus had already given ample notice of his power over demonic forces. He only had to be in their vicinity to make them tremble. On one occasion, a man implored him to heal his only son:

> On the next day, when they had come down from the
> mountain, a great crowd met him. And behold, a man
> from the crowd cried out, "Teacher, I beg you to look
> at my son, for he is my only child. And behold, a spirit
> seizes him, and he suddenly cries out. It convulses him
> so that he foams at the mouth, and shatters him, and will
> hardly leave him. And I begged your disciples to cast it
> out, but they could not." Jesus answered, "O faithless
> and twisted generation, how long am I to be with you
> and bear with you? Bring your son here." While he was
> coming, the demon threw him to the ground and con-
> vulsed him. But Jesus rebuked the unclean spirit and
> healed the boy, and gave him back to his father. And all
> were astonished at the majesty of God (Luke 9:37-43).

Later Jesus commissioned seventy of his disciples to go out and
exercise the same healing ministry. They came back, Luke said, "with
joy, saying, 'Lord, even the demons are subject to us in your name'"
(Luke 10:17). At which point Jesus immediately reminded them that
Satan's helplessness in the presence of God is nothing new:

> And he said to them, "I saw Satan fall like lightning from
> heaven. Behold, I have given you authority to tread on
> serpents and scorpions, and over all the power of the
> enemy, and nothing shall hurt you. Nevertheless, do not
> rejoice in this, that the spirits are subject to you, but
> rejoice that your names are written in heaven" (Luke
> 10:18-20).

By the time of the Crucifixion, then, Satan had already been
given a foretaste of his final defeat. But it was only a foretaste.

In his first coming Jesus bound the demonic powers by releasing
some men and women from physical infirmity, including opening
the eyes of the blind, the ears of the deaf, and loosing the tongues
of the mute. But in his *second* coming he is going to release *all* of his
children from their infirmities.

> By the time of the Crucifixion, Satan had already
> been given a foretaste of his final defeat.

In his first coming those few people Jesus raised from the dead eventually had to die again. But at his *second* coming he is going to raise *all* of his children to live forevermore.

In his first coming Jesus delivered as many demon-possessed people as were brought to him. But in his *second* coming he is going to free *all* of his children from satanic oppression and depression.

Again, Jesus gave the clue before his death and resurrection. In the parable of the wheat and the weeds, an enemy came and sowed weeds in a farmer's wheat field. The farmer's servants offered to go and pull up the weeds, but the farmer told them not to because in doing so they would almost certainly uproot the wheat as well. Instead, he said, the servants should wait until both wheat and weeds were fully grown, and then harvest the weeds first and burn them. In the same way, Jesus explained,

> "Just as the weeds are gathered and burned with fire, so will it be at the end of the age. The Son of Man will send his angels, and they will gather out of his kingdom all causes of sin and all law-breakers, and throw them into the fiery furnace. In that place there will be weeping and gnashing of teeth. Then the righteous will shine like the sun in the kingdom of their Father. He who has ears, let him hear" (Matthew 13:40-43).

Obviously this is not Satan's favorite Scripture. In fact, in many churches today it's not fashionable to believe in hell—and if you must believe in it, for goodness' sake, don't talk about it!

Why Talk About Hell?

I realize I am on difficult terrain here. The mainline churches stopped believing in hell back yonder when they stopped believing in the Bible. Now even many popular evangelical churches refuse to preach on hell because, they tell you, hellfire sermons are not seeker-friendly. They are not a good marketing strategy for churches. They do not win friends and influence people.

Hell is a taboo subject and that suits Satan just fine. Satan does not want to hear preachers telling people to get out of Satan's camp and into Jesus' camp. Satan does not want to hear preachers telling people that unless they repent and believe in Jesus Christ, they are going to spend eternity there with Satan and all his demons. Satan does not want to hear preachers warning people to escape from the eternal judgment that is coming upon the world. Satan does not want to hear preachers talking about the lake of fire prepared for him and his angels.

So soft-pedaling the truth about all these things, as all too many churches are doing, fits Satan's desires to a tee. He is not upset when people laugh at the idea of fire and brimstone and a personal devil. When people trivialize hell and treat it as a joke, the Enemy is delighted. The fewer people who take hell seriously, the more companions Satan is likely to have.

> When people treat hell as a joke, the Enemy is delighted. The fewer people who take hell seriously, the more companions Satan is likely to have.

But as much as it grieves me to disturb anyone's sleep, I can preach nothing more and nothing less than the truth of the Scripture. Am I trying to scare you into heaven? Yes, I am. I have absolutely no hesitation in scaring the socks off you, as long as that will bring you into God's kingdom. After all, unlike a blockbuster horror movie, hell is *real*. You *ought* to be scared—unless, of course, you are on God's side already, in which case death and hell will hold no terrors for you.

The great circuit-rider revivalist Peter Cartwright was warned as he entered church one Sunday morning, "Mr. Cartwright, whatever you do, be very careful what you say. President Andrew Jackson is going to be in the service today."

Cartwright said, "Fine." When he got up to preach, he said, "I am told that President Andrew Jackson is in the congregation. Well, let me tell you before I preach that President Andrew Jackson is going to hell if he does not believe in Jesus Christ."

People were aghast. They were horrified. They didn't know where to look. And after the service most of them left the building with their chins in the air.

But not the president. Andrew Jackson walked up to Cartwright, shook his hand warmly, and said, "Sir, I want to tell you this morning that if I had a hundred men like you in my regiment, I could take on the world."

What Does the Bible Tell Us About Hell?

The Bible contains several snapshots of hell. One of them comes in Jesus' parable of the sheep and the goats. Remember that the sheep were distinguished from the goats on the basis of the way they treated "the least of these my brothers" (Matthew 25:40). As Jesus explained, the sheep on the King's right hand were the righteous, accepted into eternal life for ministering to the sick, the stranger, and the prisoner. By contrast, the goats assembled on the King's left hand made the mistake of doing exactly the opposite. Said Jesus:

> "Then he will say to those on his left, 'Depart from me,
> you cursed, into the eternal fire prepared for the devil
> and his angels'" (Matthew 25:41).

The same picture of hell—as a place of everlasting fire—can be found in the parable of the rich man and Lazarus, and also in Revelation. But Matthew's picture of the sheep and the goats tells us something important. Although unbelievers will end up in the lake of fire, the lake of fire was *not made for them*. It was made for Satan and his angels and existed long before the creation of Adam. Even now it is waiting. John describes the upcoming event through eyes of faith, which are able to see the future as a present reality:

> The devil who had deceived them was thrown into the lake of fire and sulfur where the beast and the false prophet were, and they will be tormented day and night forever and ever (Revelation 20:10).

Notice something else. The Bible makes it clear that hell is a literal place. It is not a state of mind, not a figment of the imagination, not a literary device. No—hell is a real place, just like Washington, DC, or Paris, or Honolulu. To read the text in any other way is to indulge in wishful thinking.

> The Bible makes it clear that hell is a literal place. It is not a state of mind, not a figment of the imagination, not a literary device.

Jesus was also explicit about the intense suffering of those who are going to be there. He emphasized that there is no return from hell and it imposes eternal separation from loved ones—eternal separation, in fact, from all that is good and holy, including God himself.

Jesus talked about these things not because he delighted in them, but because he was warning us. Knowing that hell exists, and knowing what hell is like, helps us not to end up going there. The last thing God wants is for anyone else to follow Satan into everlasting punishment.

But if hell is a literal place, is it also *literally* an eternally burning lake? Twenty-one places in the Bible, all in the New Testament, refer to hell as a place of unquenched fire. Some people consider that the only truth worth having is literal truth, and insist that if the

Bible talks about hell as a lake of fire, then it must be exactly that. In response their critics have pointed out that, since the earth, and indeed the universe, contains a finite quantity of combustible material, sooner or later a literal hell would run out of fuel. Some of them have even tried to calculate how many millions of years will elapse before this happens. If hell can burn only as long as its fires can be fed, they argue, it is not *eternal*.

I believe this whole argument is a waste of time. The Bible is full of expressions God does not expect us to take literally. To pick an example at random, it would be doing a disservice to the Scriptures to insist that the "woman clothed with the sun" in Revelation 12:1 is literally wearing the sun like a pair of jeans. That is not how John meant us to understand him. In this and many other instances, the Bible uses a figure of speech to illustrate a principle, and there are two things we need to remember about this use of figurative language and symbols.

First, *symbols in the Bible are not meant to blur an issue or diminish its importance*. That a passage or a phrase is symbolic does not make it any less true. It simply alerts us to the fact that some spiritual realities cannot be described directly or by literal means. The truth lies so far beyond our ordinary experience that using symbols or figures of speech is the only way to help our finite minds grasp it.

Second, it is important to remember that *the thing being symbolized is always greater than the symbol*. Let me give you an example. Twice a month at my church we have a Communion table bearing some bread and some wine. We say that the bread represents the body of the Lord Jesus Christ. It is not *in fact* the body of the Lord Jesus Christ, because the body of the Lord Jesus Christ is in heaven. He is already there at the right hand of the Father. But the bread serves to remind us of the body of Christ. God accommodates our finite minds.

This is exactly what is happening in Revelation when we read about streets of gold and gates studded with precious stones. Is God putting a commercial value on heaven? Not at all. He is finding things in our own world that will help us visualize things in a world we have never seen.

In the same way, the phrase "lake of fire" is not meant to be taken at face value. Hell is something other than a literal lake of fire, and actually something much worse. Were we able to take a photograph of hell, it might not look at all like a lake or like fire—nevertheless "lake of fire" is the expression in our language that conveys more accurately than any other how it feels to be there.

The Anatomy of Hell

Fire is not the only idea the Bible uses to describe hell. Four more symbols show us what kind of place hell is and what a terrible fate it is to be trapped inside it:

1. Confinement

The parable of the unforgiving servant (Matthew 18:21-35) pictures hell as a prison. But hell is not like a physical prison. Earthly prisons confine the body, but not the soul or the mind. Earthly prisons cannot chain down the spirit. No matter what happens to the body, the spirit is free to worship, free to create, free to imagine, free to anticipate, free to hope.

When Paul and Silas were beaten up and thrown into the Philippian jail, they were suffering some of the worst privations a human prison has to offer. Nevertheless they were singing and praising God. Physical confinement could not repress their joy in the Lord. They took Jesus' words in Matthew to heart: "And do not fear those who kill the body but cannot kill the soul" (10:28).

But there is a second and more chilling part to Jesus' saying: "Rather fear him who can destroy both soul and body in hell" (10:28). Hell locks up not only flesh and blood but also imagination, thought, creativity, hope. And it does so permanently.

> Hell locks up not only flesh and blood
> but also imagination, thought, creativity,
> hope. And it does so permanently.

Prisoners in Venice were once housed in a building accessed by a single bridge over a canal. The bridge, which still stands, is called the Bridge of Sighs—for no prisoner going across it ever crossed back the other way.

Hell keeps its victims, and it makes Sing Sing look like a Scout camp!

2. Darkness

John said in Revelation that the new City of God will need no created light because Jesus himself will illuminate it. Jesus is the light of the world.

In contrast, hell is portrayed as a place of perpetual blackness. "Bind him hand and foot and cast him into the outer darkness," the king ordered his servants in the parable of the wedding feast— thus consigning to hell the man who had stolen into the celebration (Matthew 22:13). Similarly, in the parable of the talents, the king ordered, "And cast the worthless servant into the outer darkness" (Matthew 25:30).

In one way this darkness is literal, for hell has no morning or evening, no twilights or glorious sunsets. But the darkness is also moral and spiritual. The intruder to the wedding feast and the unprofitable servant are both *excluded* from the places where they had once belonged. Hell is a place where things *do not* happen, a place of benightedness, dullness, and ignorance. There is no light for reading, but there is also no newspaper to read, no news at all.

3. Suffering

The wedding intruder and the unprofitable servant encountered "weeping and gnashing of teeth" in the outer darkness. Hell is a place of terrible suffering, a place of constant agony. There is no relief, not for one second.

Jesus told the story of the rich man and the beggar Lazarus, whose fortunes were reversed after death so that Lazarus was carried by angels to Abraham's bosom while the rich man roasted in hell.

> "The rich man also died and was buried, and in Hades, being in torment, he lifted up his eyes and saw Abraham far off and Lazarus at his side. And he called out, 'Father Abraham, have mercy on me, and send Lazarus to dip the end of his finger in water and cool my tongue, for I am in anguish in this flame'" (Luke 16:22-24).

4. Loneliness

It is often said that people who go to hell will at least be in good company. George Bernard Shaw once commented that all of the interesting people will be in hell. The apostle John gives a short list of these interesting people: "But as for the cowardly, the faithless, the detestable, as for murderers, the sexually immoral, sorcerers, idolaters, and all liars, their portion will be in the lake that burns with fire and sulfur, which is the second death" (Revelation 21:8).

There are no personal relationships in hell. It is solitary confinement.

Well, I would not invite these people to *my* birthday party. And it is unlikely that in hell you would enjoy the company of this dubious crew for there is no fellowship in hell. One of its characteristics is the absolute isolation of each individual. C.S. Lewis once said there are no personal relationships in hell. It is solitary confinement. Once there, all feelings of attachment, of friendship, and of love will be forgotten forever.

With stakes this high, it is no wonder we are fighting in the invisible war. But there is coming a day when we will fight no more battles.

LOOKING AHEAD

We need to know our Enemy—to understand him, to outmaneuver him, to keep out of his reach, and to drive him away. But at the same time we should not get our priorities out of order. We should not pay Satan the compliment of thinking about him so much that he comes to dominate our lives. We need to be sober and vigilant.

Yet we also need to be oriented to the positive. We need to keep our eyes on Jesus, the author and finisher of our faith. For the closer we are to him, and the more we appreciate and come to value the good things of God's kingdom, the more natural it will be for us to reject the devil's temptations and to live in the Spirit.

One of my friends and church members died some time ago. He knew he was about to die, and in the last weeks of his life he dedicated himself to telling as many people as he could about heaven. Right to the end, he looked forward. He said, "I've been religious all my life, but on March 28, 1995, Jesus came into my life for the first time." He told all his friends. He told all his family. It was so exciting to see somebody looking forward to heaven. He had the right perspective.

In the end, you can't compare the thrill of heaven with the horrors of hell.

THE PROMISE OF HEAVEN

So what reward does God have for those who fight in his army? Just what is it like in heaven, where God's people will reign once the battle is over?

Some say that heaven is just a state of mind, and those who say this are often the same people who tell us the identical lie about hell. Heaven, they say, is an abstract idea. Wishful thinking. A figure of speech.

To those pessimistic people I want to say, loud and clear, that heaven is a real place. In John 14, Jesus said so. He uses the Greek word *topos*, which means exactly that. A place. A location. Jesus told his disciples,

> "Let not your hearts be troubled. Believe in God; believe
> also in me. In my Father's house are many rooms. If it
> were not so, would I have told you that I go to prepare a
> place for you?" (14:1-2).

Jesus existed in heaven for eternity prior to his incarnation, therefore what he says about heaven should be enough.

But many others saw heaven. Let me give you some examples.

Just before he was martyred, Stephen, one of the first deacons of the church, said, "Behold, I see the heavens opened, and the Son of Man standing at the right hand of God" (Acts 7:56).

And John, the apostle God chose to give a brief glimpse into eternity, said, "After this I looked, and there before me was a door standing open in heaven" (Revelation 4:1 NIV).

No abstract idea. No figure of speech. Heaven is a real place with real people who have real bodies. Real life and real joy. Real peace. There are even real angels there.

And that is where my real home is. In fact, all the soldiers in God's army are going there.

The Bible gives us six descriptions of our life in heaven:

1. We Shall Have Uninterrupted Fellowship with God

Someone once asked D.L. Moody, "What are you expecting to do when you get to heaven?"

"I expect to spend the first thousand years looking at Jesus," he replied.

I am not excited by the pearly gates and the streets of gold, whatever they are. Like Moody, I am excited about spending years just looking at Jesus. The apostle Paul knew that this would happen: "For now we see in a mirror dimly, but then face to face" (1 Corinthians 13:12).

I will see my Lord face-to-face! And so will you.

I will see my Lord face-to-face! And so will you.

After Jesus told his disciples he was going to prepare a place for them, he promised them,

> "And if I go and prepare a place for you, I will come again and will take you to myself, that where I am you may be also" (John 14:3).

Heaven would not be heaven without Jesus and without the ability to fellowship with him forever.

2. We Shall Rest from the Battle

Heaven is a real place—a place of rest. In describing his vision of heaven, John said,

> And I heard a voice from heaven saying, "Write this: Blessed are the dead who die in the Lord from now on." "Blessed indeed," says the Spirit, "that they may rest from their labors, for their deeds follow them!" (Revelation 14:13).

Some people think this means that we are going to be idle in heaven. That may be the vision of the Great Society, but that was not John's vision. He did not see us lying on fluffy clouds and strumming harps. Far from it!

Yet we will rest from the spiritual battle against Satan and the world. We will no longer have to fight temptations and the devil. We will not have to struggle constantly to keep the world from squeezing us into its mold.

The rest in heaven is similar to the Bible's concept of the Sabbath. Unfortunately this earthly day of rest is one of the most misunderstood commandments. The Sabbath was not created to play golf or tennis or to go to the beach. (I don't mean to step on any toes here, but that's just not the biblical concept.)

God set aside the Sabbath so we can take our minds off the mundane and humdrum activity of our lives—in order to focus on him. It is to be a Sabbath unto the Lord.

Remember what Jesus told the Pharisees when they were so concerned that his disciples had broken the law by picking some heads of wheat on the Sabbath. Picking grain, they said, was work, and work was forbidden on the Sabbath. And Jesus explained to them, "The Sabbath was made for man, not man for the Sabbath. So the Son of Man is lord even of the Sabbath" (Mark 2:27-28).

The Sabbath is set aside because God knows we will otherwise get busy and work hard—and leave God out. So the Sabbath is a day we focus on God for twenty-four hours out of the week. We focus only on God—his holiness, his majesty, his dominion, his power, his mercy, his grace.

> We will go from the secular to the sacred, from the humdrum to the holy, from the mundane to the majestic—not just one day a week, but all the time.

And when the Bible talks about rest in eternity, that is exactly what we will do. We will go from the secular to the sacred, from the humdrum to the holy, from the mundane to the majestic—not just one day a week, but all the time.

3. We Will Serve the Lord

Heaven is a real place, a place of rest, and a place where we will serve our Lord. John also said about heaven,

> No longer will there be any curse. The throne of God and of the Lamb will be in the city, and his servants will serve him. They will see his face, and his name will be on their foreheads (Revelation 22:3-4 NIV).

The Greek word translated "serve" here, *latreuo*, indicates that there will be joyful service, enthusiastic service, voluntary service to the Lord God. Whatever the service, it will not be a chore. It will not be accompanied by fatigue. Our service will come from our gratitude to God for redeeming us, for getting us into heaven in the first place.

The Bible gives an indication that this service includes reigning and ruling with God. Have you thought about this?

In Matthew 25 the master told the faithful laborer:

> "Well done, good and faithful servant; you have been faithful over a few things, I will make you ruler over many things" (25:23 NKJV).

Whether I receive one dollar or ten trillion dollars to manage in this life does not make any difference, because God owns it all. What does matter is how faithful I have been with what God has given me.

And what about you? Will the Lord say these words to you: "Well done, good and faithful servant"?

4. We Will Have Full Knowledge

Heaven is a real place, a place of rest, a place of service, and a place where we will know and understand all things. After Paul told the Corinthian Christians, "For now we see in a mirror dimly, but then face to face," he added, "Now I know in part; then I shall know fully, even as I have been fully known" (1 Corinthians 13:12).

How often we hear questions like, "Why does God allow bad things to happen to good people?"

On earth I don't know why diseases, war, and suffering occur. In heaven I shall understand it all. Here I don't know why earthquakes and hurricanes happen. But there I shall understand it all. I shall see things so clearly from God's perspective, there will be no need even to ask questions.

And I don't believe for a moment that anyone will be able to say, "God, you did not give me a fair chance"—especially those who rejected him.

5. We Will Be in a Place of Continuous Glory

A real place, a place of rest, a place of service, a place where we will know all, and a place of continuous glory.

If you do not spend time looking to heaven now, something is wrong with your faith. You are not living the victorious life, the life Paul described to the Corinthians.

The apostle Paul did not teach God's Word in an air-conditioned sanctuary. In Ephesus, for instance, he could rent a hall only when the philosophers were not using it, and they had all the halls reserved during the morning and evening, the cool of the day. So Paul could teach only in the middle of the day, in the sweltering heat, at a time when everybody else was resting.

Several times soldiers lashed Paul's back. People stoned him. The Romans persecuted him, as did the Jews. Some Christians who could not forget how he had persecuted them before his conversion on the road to Damascus even hated him. In all of this, he focused on heaven so he could withstand the pressures of earth:

> So we do not lose heart. Though our outer self is wasting away, our inner self is being renewed day by day. For this light momentary affliction is preparing for us an eternal weight of glory beyond all comparison, as we look not to the things that are seen but to the things that are unseen.

For the things that are seen are transient, but the things that are unseen are eternal (2 Corinthians 4:16-18).

In heaven God's character will be so revealed in us, we will be transformed to be like him.

The word *glory* in this passage refers to the revelation of the character of God in Jesus Christ. In heaven God's character will be so revealed in us, we will be transformed to be like him. The apostle Paul told the Colossian Christians:

> If then you have been raised with Christ, seek the things that are above, where Christ is, seated at the right hand of God. Set your minds on things that are above, not on things that are on earth. For you have died, and your life is hidden with Christ in God. When Christ who is your life appears, then you also will appear with him in glory (Colossians 3:1-4).

6. We Will Be in Constant Worship

And, finally, heaven is a place where we will be in constant worship. Please, whenever you think of worship in heaven, do not be tempted to equate it with the average eleven o'clock Sunday morning worship service in the average dead church.

I was once told about one of the most prominent citizens of England, who confessed to Lord Riddle, "When I was a young man, the thought of heaven was more frightening to me than the thought of hell…I pictured heaven as a place where time would be perpetual Sundays, with perpetual eleven a.m. services from which there would be no escape. It was a horrible nightmare that made me an atheist for ten years."

Instead of the average Sunday morning service, think of worship as it is described in Revelation 19. The book of Revelation gives us a picture of the exuberance and excitement and unspeakable joy of worship in heaven. John said,

> After this I heard what seemed to be the loud voice of a
> great multitude in heaven, crying out,
> "Hallelujah!
> Salvation and glory and power belong to our God,
> for his judgments are true and just…"
> And the twenty-four elders and the four living creatures
> fell down and worshiped God who was seated on the
> throne, saying, "Amen. Hallelujah!" And from the
> throne came a voice saying,
> "Praise our God,
> all you his servants,
> you who fear him,
> small and great."
> (Revelation 19:1-2,4-5)

I can only imagine the sound and sight of all believers of all ages—Old Testament saints, New Testament saints, saints from all the ages—together with the myriad of angels and musicians, all worshiping the Lord, who is right there in the center of them all. Imagine the shouts of hallelujah and the amens punctuating the crescendo of heavenly singers and the fanfare of celestial trumpets.

I can only imagine the sound and sight of all
believers of all ages together with the myriad of
angels and musicians, all worshiping the Lord.

In *The Problem of Pain*, C.S. Lewis said of heaven,

> All the things that have ever deeply possessed your soul
> have been but hints of it—tantalizing glimpses, prom-
> ises never quite fulfilled, echoes that died away just as

they caught your ear. But if it should really become man-
ifest—if there ever came an echo that did not die away
but swelled into the sound itself—you would know it.
Beyond all possibility of doubt you would say, "Here at
last is the thing I was made for." People wondered what
he meant, until he went on to say,

We will praise you with our two eyes, by looking only
to you. We will exalt you with our two ears, by listening
only to your voice. We will extol you with our two hands,
by working in your service. We will honor you with our
two feet, by walking in the way of your statutes. We will
magnify you with our tongues, by bearing testimony
to your loving kindness. We will worship you with our
hearts, by loving only you. We thank you for this instrument, Lord. Keep it in tune. Play upon it as you will, and
ring out the melodies of your grace. May its harmonies
always express your glory.

I look forward to seeing you there. Keep up the faith!

NOTES

1. www.techaddiction.ca/files/porn-addiction-statistics.jpg.

2. www.techaddiction.ca/files/porn-addiction-stats.jpg.

3. www.covenanteyes.com/pornstats/.

4. "Viewing pornography is not an emotionally or physiologically neutral experience. It is fundamentally different from looking at black-and-white photos of the Lincoln Memorial or taking in a color map of the provinces of Canada...Porn is vicarious and voyeuristic at its core, but it is also something more. Porn is a whispered promise...Time spent with porn prevents the user from engaging in real relationships with real people who can better meet their needs" (William M. Struthers, *Wired for Intimacy: How Pornography Hijacks the Male Brain* (Downers Grove, IL: IVP Books, 2010), Kindle location 614).

5. "Over time these neural paths become wider as they are repeatedly traveled with each exposure to pornography. They become the automatic pathway through which interactions with women are routed. The neural circuitry anchors this process solidly in the brain. With each lingering stare, pornography deepens a Grand Canyon-like gorge in the brain through which images of women are destined to flow. This extends to women that they have not seen naked or engaging in sexual acts as well. All women become potential porn stars in the minds of these men. They have unknowingly created a neurological circuit that imprisons their ability to see women rightly as created in God's image" (Ibid., Kindle location 790).

6. Paul Bedard, "Study: Watching Porn Boosts Support for Same-Sex Marriage," *Washington Examiner*, February 4, 2013 (http://washingtonexaminer.com/study-watching-porn-boosts-support-for-same-sex-marriage/article/2520461).

7. NT Greek Lexicon (www.biblestudytools.com/lexicons/greek/kjv/porneia.html).

8. NT Greek Lexicon (www.biblestudytools.com/lexicons/greek/kjv/pheugo.html).

Michael Youssef was born in Egypt and lived in Lebanon and Australia before coming to the United States. He has degrees from Australia and the US, and he earned a PhD in social anthropology from Emory University. Michael served for nearly ten years with the Haggai Institute, traveling around the world teaching leadership principles. He rose to the position of managing director at the age of thirty-one, and the family settled in Atlanta.

Dr. Youssef founded The Church of The Apostles in 1987 with fewer than forty adults with the mission to "equip the saints and seek the lost." The church has since grown to a congregation of over three thousand. This church on a hill was the launching pad for Leading The Way, an international ministry whose radio and television programs are heard by millions at home and abroad.

For more on Michael Youssef, The Church of The Apostles, and Leading The Way, visit apostles.org and www.leadingtheway.org.

The Leadership Style of Jesus

How to Make a Lasting Impact

No matter what leadership arena you serve in—whether leading a family, a church, a civic organization, a company—adopting the leadership example of Jesus will make you more effective and productive. Leadership is influence, and no leader has had greater influence on the world than Jesus Christ. The lessons of his leadership style are practical, learnable skills that you can apply today.

Michael Youssef, who has executive experience in worldwide ministries, has examined the leadership Jesus modeled and suggests Christlike qualities every leader needs. But he doesn't stop there. With Jesus as the standard, Dr. Youssef considers how to deal with the temptations and pressures leaders face, including

- anger
- loneliness
- criticism
- the use of power
- passing the torch to others

If you are in search of excellence in developing your leadership abilities, you will find much to aid your quest in this close-up look at Jesus—the greatest leader who ever lived.

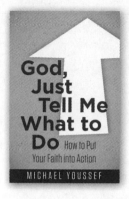

God, Just Tell Me What to Do

How to Put Your Faith into Action

God is constantly teaching us through our daily experiences. He wants us to master today's challenges and to be equipped to take on even greater challenges tomorrow. He wants our lives to reveal the reality of our growing faith and godly character.

In *God, Just Tell Me What to Do,* Dr. Michael Youssef offers biblical wisdom and encouragement to help you live out your Christian faith in such important areas as

- using your resources wisely
- thriving through trials and temptations
- understanding and obeying the Word of God
- guarding against the pressures of culture
- taming your tongue

As you learn to put your faith into action as a follower of Christ, you will discover depths of strength, courage, and joy you never knew were waiting for you.

Leading the Way Through the Bible Commentary Series

About the Series: The Leading the Way Through the Bible commentary series will not only increase your Bible knowledge, but it will motivate you to apply God's Word to the problems of our hurting world and to a deeper and more obedient walk with Jesus Christ. The writing is lively, informal, and packed with stories that illustrate the truth of God's Word. The Leading the Way series is a call to action—and a call to the exciting adventure of living for Christ.

Books in this series:

Leading the Way Through Joshua
Leading the Way Through Daniel
Leading the Way Through Galatians
Leading the Way Through Ephesians

To learn more about Harvest House books and
to read sample chapters, visit our website:

www.harvesthousepublishers.com

HARVEST HOUSE PUBLISHERS
EUGENE, OREGON